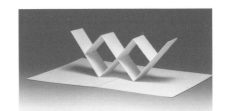

Paper Magic
Pop-up Paper Craft

ORIGAMIC ARCHITECTURE BY MASAHIRO CHATANI

PaperMagic
Pop-up Paper Craft

CONTENTS

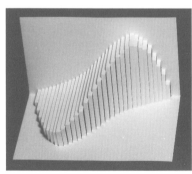

Flowers and Animals

Monthly Cards

Basics in Origamic Architecture

Message from the author

My paper craftsmanship was just an avocation at my spare time, but, unexpectedly, Mercury smiles upon my work and thanks to an increasing market demand, it has taken shape as the fourth volume of "The world of Paper Magic".
Co-authored with Ms. Keiko Nakazawa, the title deals with every nature item and creature.
Work done with super dexterity concerns with those around the globe from antiquity to space-age.

Author: Masahiro Chatani

1967: Doctor of Engineering
1977: Visiting Associate Professor, University of Washington at Seattle
1980~ : Professor, Tokyo Institute of Technology

★ Published by ONDORISHA PUBLISHERS, LTD., 11-11 Nishigoken-cho, Shinjuku-ku, Tokyo 162, Japan.
★ Sole Overseas Distributor: Japan Publications Trading Co., Ltd.
P.O. Box 5030 Tokyo International, Tokyo, Japan
★ Distributed
in United States by Kodansha America, Inc.
114 Fifth Avenue, New York, NY 10011, U.S.A.
in Canada by Fitzhenry & Whiteside LTD.
195 Allstate Parkway, Markham, Ontario L3R 4T8, Canada
in British Isles & European Continent by Premier Book Marketing Ltd.,
1 Gower Street, London WC1E 6HA, England
in Australia by Bookwise International
54 Crittenden Road, Findon, South Australia 5023, Australia
in The Far East and Japan by Japan Publications Trading Co, Ltd.
1-2-1, Sarugaku-cho, Chiyoda-ku, Tokyo 101, Japan

10

ISBN 0-87040-757-0
Printed in Japan

Castles and Palaces

①OSAKA Castle
Instructions on page 36.

②HIMEJI Castle
Instructions on page 37.

③**NAGOYA Castle**
Instructions on page 38.

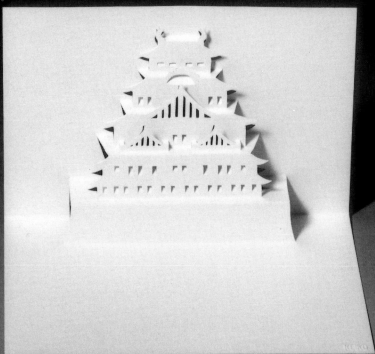

④**UWAJIMA Castle**
Instructions on page 26.

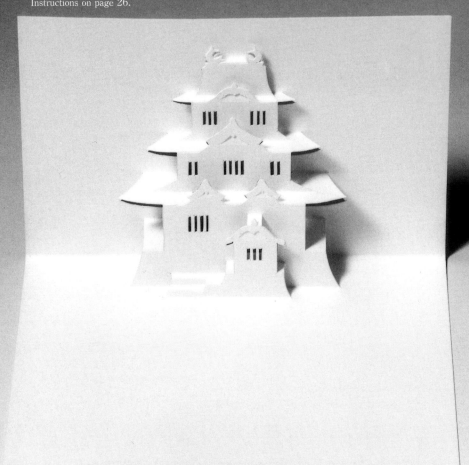

⑤Chateau Chenonceau
Instructions on page 39.

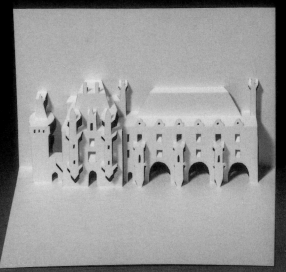

⑥Chateau d'Azay-le-Rideau
Instructions on page 40.

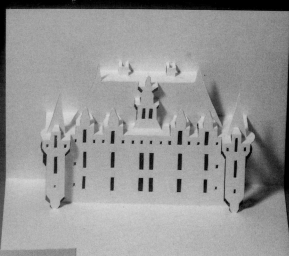

⑦Schloss Neuschwanstein
Instructions on page 41.

⑧Milano Duomo
Instructions on page 42.

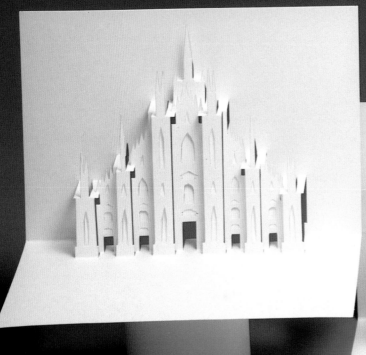

⑨Salon Rico
Instructions on page 43.

⑩Alhambra Granada Court of Lions
Instructions on page 44.

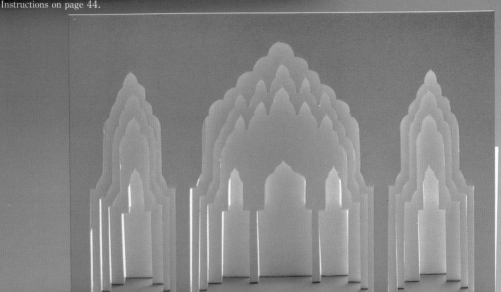

8

⑪**Mecca**
Instructions on page 85.

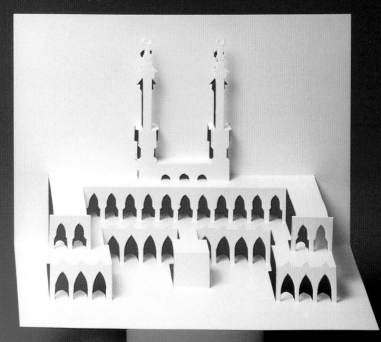

⑫**Medina**
Instructions on page 45.

9

⑬**Wave**
Instructions on page 46.

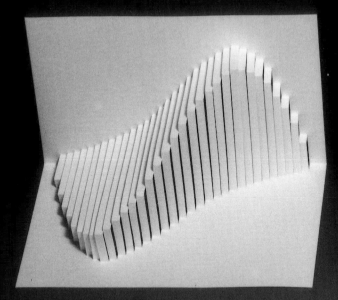

⑭**Stairs**
Instructions on page 88.

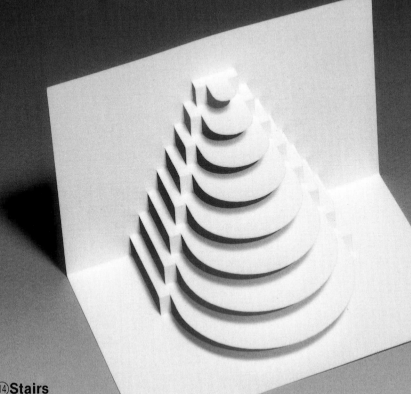

⑮Wall
Instructions on page 89.

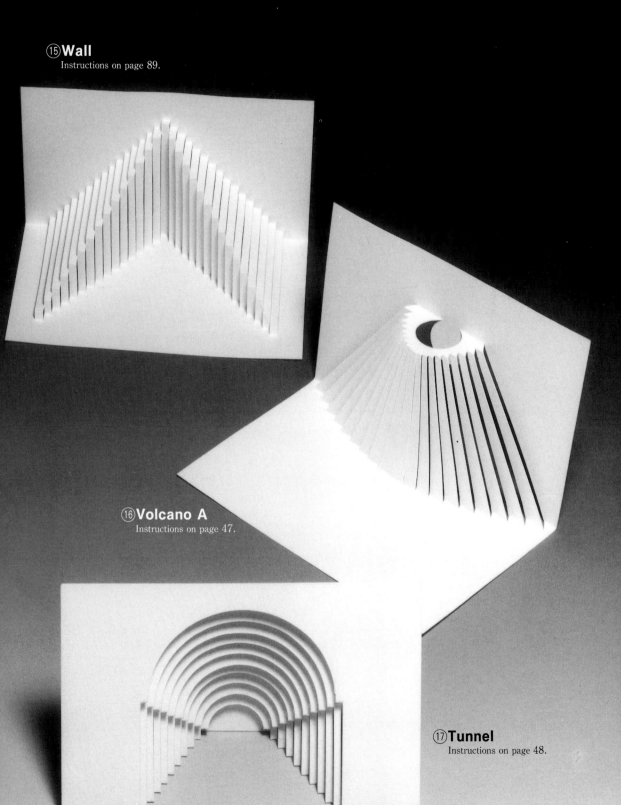

⑯Volcano A
Instructions on page 47.

⑰Tunnel
Instructions on page 48.

⑱Circling
Instructions on page 32.

⑲Cedars
Instructions on page 49.

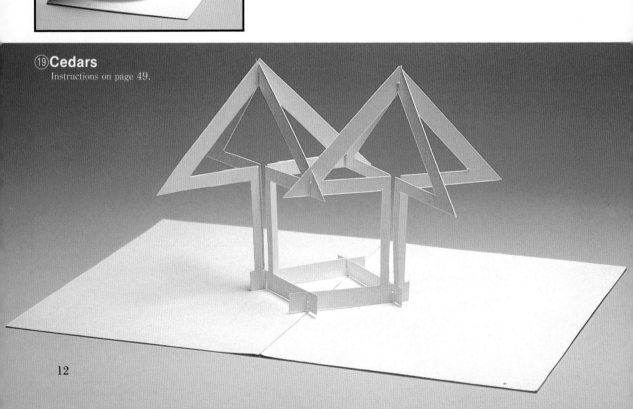

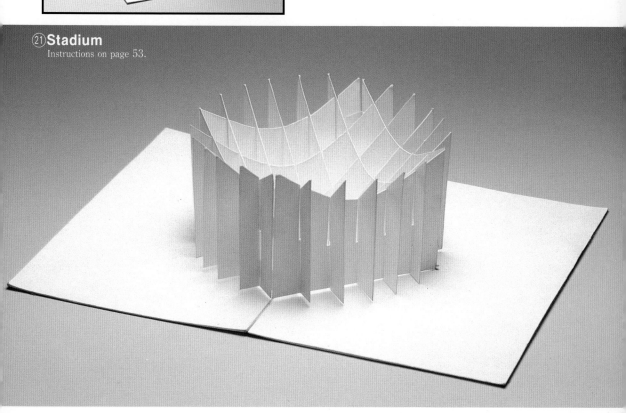

⑳ Cone
Instructions on page 51.

㉑ Stadium
Instructions on page 53.

㉒Cross of W

Instructions on page 55.

㉓Friends

Instructions on page 56.

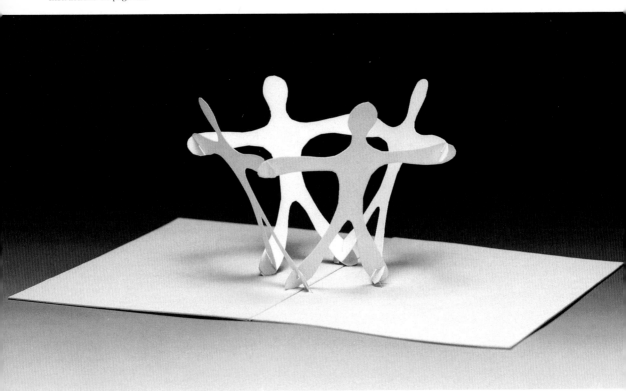

㉔**Slanted Lozenge**
Instructions on page 57.

㉕**Volcano B**
Instructions on page 58.

Flowers and Animals

㉖ X mas Tree
Instructions on page 92.

㉗ Ballerina
Instructions on page 59.

㉘ Tree of Life
Instructions on page 60.

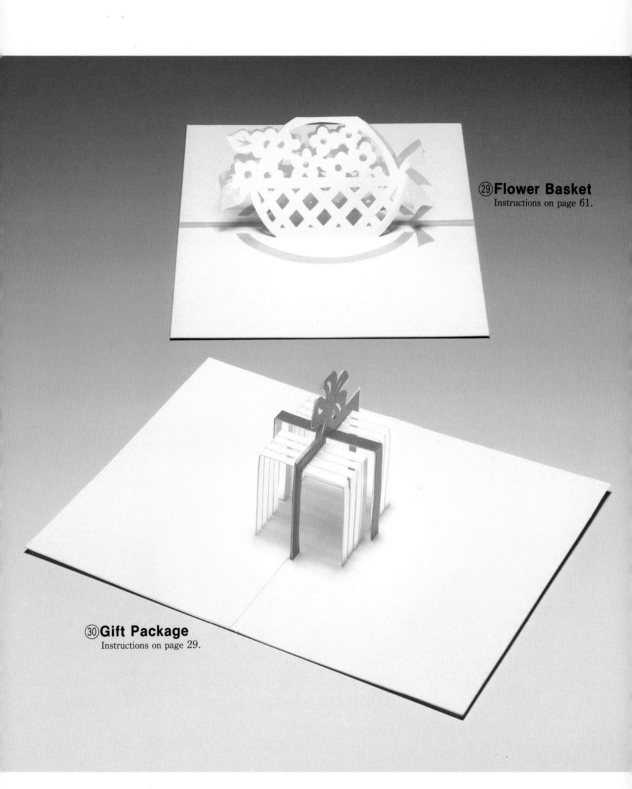

㉙**Flower Basket**
Instructions on page 61.

㉚**Gift Package**
Instructions on page 29.

㉛ Morning glory
Instructions on page 62.

㉜ Tulip
Instructions on page 63.

㉝**Bouquet**
Instructions on page 64.

㉞**Camellia**
Instructions on page 66.

㉟**Sunflower**
Instructions on page 65.

㊱**Rabbit A**
Instructions on page 68.

㊲**Crane & Pine**
Instructions on page 69.

㊳**Butterfly**
Instructions on page 70.

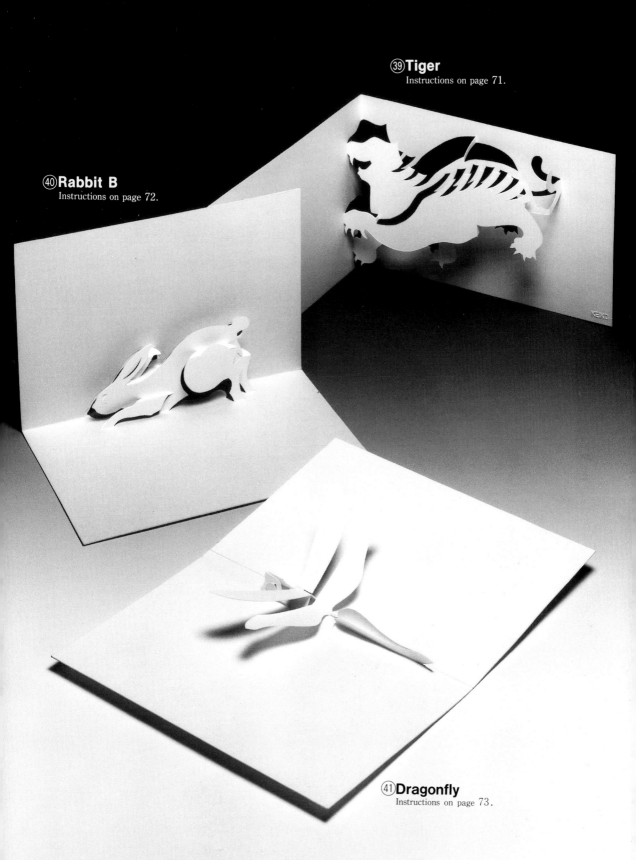

㊴**Tiger**
Instructions on page 71.

㊵**Rabbit B**
Instructions on page 72.

㊶**Dragonfly**
Instructions on page 73.

Monthly Cards

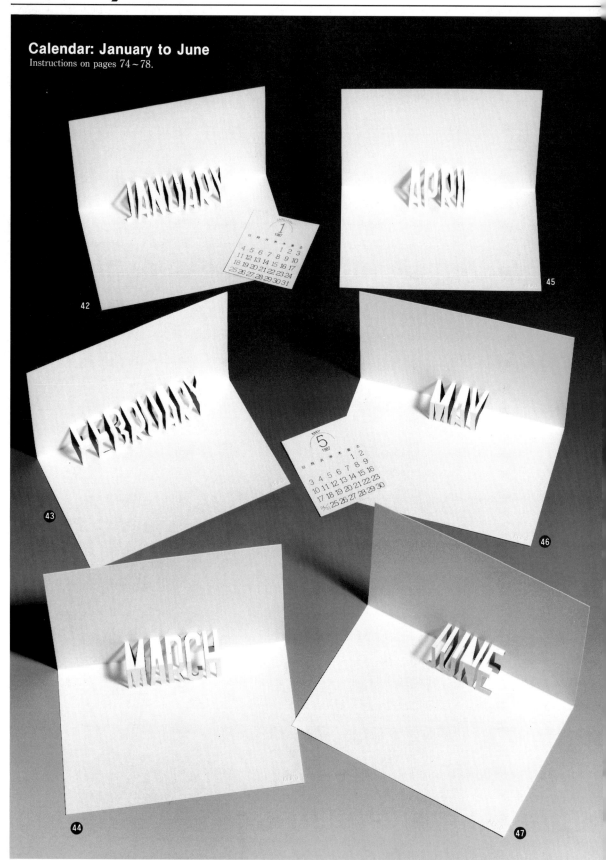

Calendar: January to June
Instructions on pages 74~78.

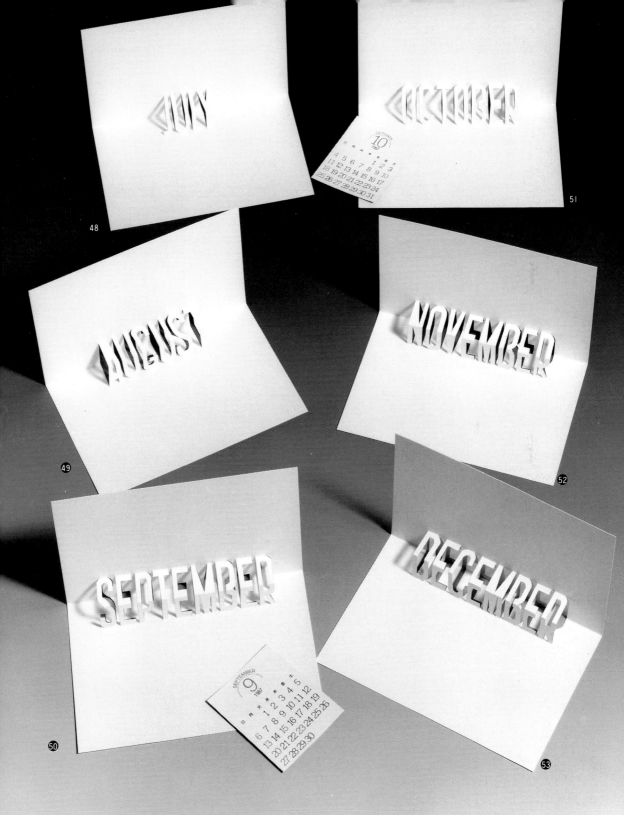

Basics in Origamic Architecture

Materials and Tools

All the works shown in this book can be made with simple materials and tools. Your hands and head are the most important tools. However, the following materials and tools are required for the best results

To make the 90° open type card:

1. Kent paper (To make a sample, use drawing paper or graph paper.)
2. Sketch pad
3. Graph paper (1mm square)
4. Pencil (HB or H)
5. Eraser
6. Tracing paper
7. Clear plastic ruler
8. Steel ruler
9. Protractor
10. Cutting knife (Circle cutter works well for curves.)
11. Thick and thin stylus pen
12. Clear adhesive tape
13. Compasses
14. Pointed tweezers
15. All-purpose glue
16. Drafting tape

To make the new 180° open type card:

The following papers are required in addition to those above.

1. Kent paper for the base. Make sure of cutting into the indicated size.
2. Colored construction paper for decoration.

To make the ordinary 180° open type card:

In addition to those above for the 90° open type card, the following materials are required.

1. Kent paper for the base.
2. Kent paper for backing.
3. Japanese rice paper for reinforcement.
4. White cotton thread for attaching parts onto the base.

About the paper:

All the cards in this book are made of medium-weight white Kent paper in double postcard size. For the 90° open type card, use one sheet of 20cm by 15cm ($7\frac{7}{8}'' \times 5\frac{7}{8}''$) white Kent paper. For the ordinary 180° type card, use two sheets of 20cm by 15cm ($7\frac{7}{8}'' \times 5\frac{7}{8}''$) for the base and backing and one sheet in different size for making a three dimensional shape. For the new 180° open type card, use one sheet of 20cm by 15cm ($7\frac{7}{8}'' \times 5\frac{7}{8}''$) for backing and one sheet in different size for the base and shape. See page 28 for handling paper.

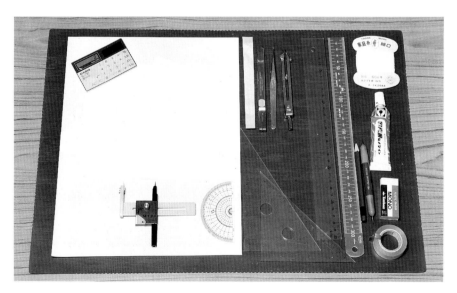

Important Points in Making Pop-up Cards

1. To make the 90° open type card:

The 90° open type cards are made by cutting and folding as indicated. The main points in making the 90° open type cards are as follows:

How to cut the pattern:

Place a traced pattern on a sheet of Kent paper and transfer the pattern by perforating with a stylus pen. Using a cutting knife and a steel ruler, cut along the perforated lines. When cutting a sharp angle, cut each side toward the point. For curves, use a circle cutter or draw curves with a pencil and cut along pencil lines free hand. Make sure that cutting is done exactly along the lines.

How to cut a sharp angle

How to crease:

A stylus pen is usually used for creasing. For a valley-fold line, score on the right side and for a moutain-fold line, score on the back. To make a neat fold line, cut at a depth of one-third of the thickness of paper on the right side. If you don't fold exactly, you may not obtain the desired shape. Begin folding from the corner of the longer fold lines using both hands. For the shorter fold lines, use the point of tweezers and fold exactly.

The base:

All the 90° open type cards are made of a sheet of paper with pop-up design. However, if you use another sheet of Kent paper of the same color or drawing paper in contrasting color for the base, an interesting effect can be added to the card. Paper of the same size as the card is often used for the base (20cm by 15cm (7⅞″×5⅞″) or 30cm by 10cm (11 ⅞″×3⅞″), etc.), but if you glue two sheets of 10cm by 15cm (3⅞″×5⅞″) paper separately onto each half of the card, you don't have to crease the center fold line and you can easily open the card. Use all-purpose glue for attaching the base. Carefully apply glue to the corners.

2. To make the 180° open type card:

It is sometimes difficult for a beginner to picture a completed three-dimensional design. However, I can say the 180° open type cards encompass all the most interesting features of pop-up designs. Please try making original cards following the instructions below.

Cut out parts:

The pattern for parts, unfolded shape and ground plan are shown for the 180° open type card. Cut the required number of parts as indicated.

Assemble the parts:

Assemble the parts following the photo. The points for assembling are given for each project, but think carefully before you start.

Attach cotton threads to the assembled parts:

The assembled parts are attached to the base at three or four places with cotton threads. Each thread is hooked onto concave part and tied or glued with a small piece of Japanese rice paper (see Circles on page 32). The places for attaching thread are indicated in the patterns. After assembling the parts, place them on the base and make sure of the exact points of attaching thread. Then, glue each thread with a small piece of Japanese rice paper.

Insert threads into holes and fix:

Insert the ends of thread (6—7cm) (2⅜—2¾″) into the holes of the base, pull thread and fix onto the base temporarily with clear adhesive tape. Check whether the assembled parts pop up when the card is opened. If it works well, fix the end of each thread with glued Japanese rice paper. Trim off excess thread.

Attach another sheet of paper for backing:

Using another sheet of white Kent paper, back the base for reinforcement and for a neater finish. If you use two sheets of 15cm by 10cm (5⅞″×3⅞″) paper, the card can be opened easily. Glue a small piece of Kent paper onto each piece of Japanese rice paper as a final touch

3. To make the new 180° open type card:

This is a combination of the 90° open type and 180° open type cards. Cut and assemble as exactly as possible. Make sure of the placement of parts when attaching them onto the backing paper.

Step-by-step Instructions for Making the 90° Open Type Card

④ **Uwajima Castle,** *shown on page 6.*

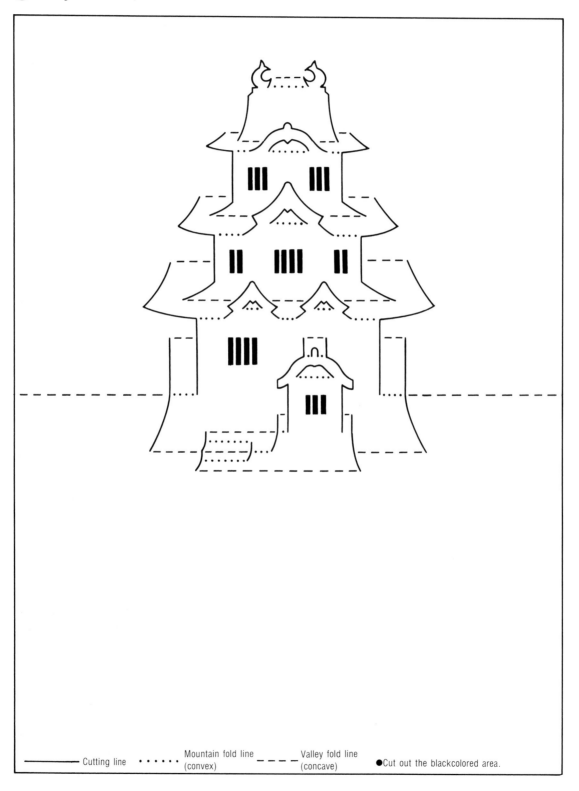

———— Cutting line ・・・・・・ Mountain fold line (convex) _ _ _ _ Valley fold line (concave) ●Cut out the blackcolored area.

①Prepare one sheet of Kent paper 15cm by 20cm (5 ⅞″×7⅞″) and the pattern traced from the opposite page.

②Place the traced pattern on Kent paper 15cm by 20cm (5⅞″×7⅞″) and fix them with Scotch tape. Perforate along the pattern with a stylus pen.

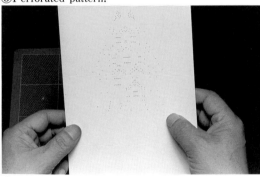

③Perforated pattern.

④Score along the mountain fold lines with a stylus pen first and then with a cutting knife cut half-way through the paper. Score along the valley fold lines on the wrong side.

⑤Cut along the cutting lines being careful not to cut beyond the lines nor to leave the uncut area (see page 25 for cutting).

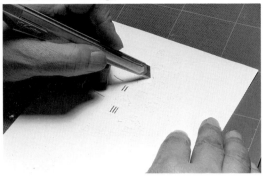

⑥Scoring and cutting have been done.

⑦Start folding by pushing the roofs forward from the wrong side with your fingers.

⑧Continue to fold the roofs in the middle.

⑨The castle pops up when the bottom parts are folded.

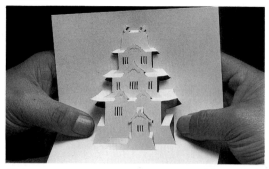

⑩Unfold to the original shape again. Then, fold along the mountain fold lines under the roofs by pushing backward with a stylus pen.

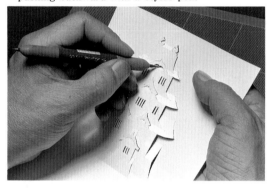

⑪Carefully fold along the creased lines angle.

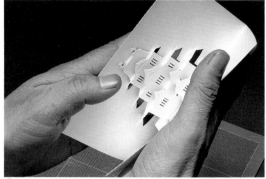

⑫When the card is opened to the right angle, the gorgeous castle appears in front of you.

How to handle paper properly:

Both Kent paper and colored construction paper are used for making pop-up cards in this book. the finished cards look neat when you handle them properly. Wood fibers have a tendency to run lengthwise in the process of making paper. Thus, most of paper has grain. When you make the 90° open type card, use the paper whose grain runs along the long side of the paper. If the paper is folded against the grain, it is at its best and stands well. On the other hand, if folded on the grain, it will curl and bend down. To find out the true grain, bend a sheet of paper of 10cm(4″) square. If the sheet is easily bent, it has a lengthwise grain. If not, it has a crosswise grain.

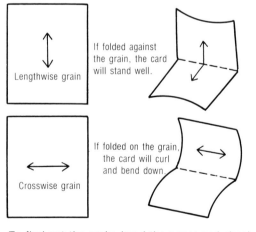

Lengthwise grain

If folded against the grain, the card will stand well.

Crosswise grain

If folded on the grain, the card will curl and bend down.

To find out the grain, bend the paper and check.

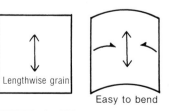

Lengthwise grain

Easy to bend   Hard to bend

30 **Gift Package,** *shown on page 17.*

① The following papers are required for the new 180° open type card. (a) White Kent paper for backing, 15cm by 20cm (5⅞″×7⅞″). (b) White Kent paper for the base and shape, 15cm by 34cm (5⅞″×13⅜″). (c) Colored construction paper for decoration, 7cm by 20cm (2¾″×7⅞″). (d) Patterns for the base, bow and package.

② Place the traced pattern A on Kent paper of 15cm by 34cm (5⅞″×13⅜″) and perforate at the corners and along curved lines with a stylus pen.

③ Cut along the cutting lines using a metal ruler and a cutting knife.

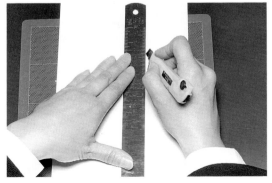

④ Cutting has been done.

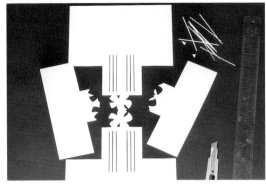

⑤ Score along the fold lines. Score the paper on the surface for the mountain fold and on the underside for the valley fold.

⑥ Place the traced pattern B on the colored construction paper and perforate at the corners and along curved lines with a stylus pen.

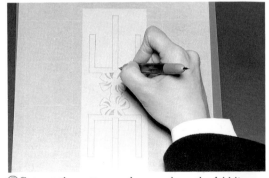

⑦ Cut out the pattern and score along the fold lines.

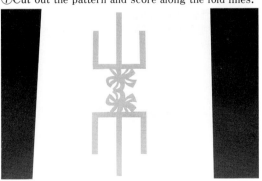

⑧Place the cut-out part B on the part A and glue them together.

⑨Fold the glued parts A and B along the fold lines.

⑩Check whether the folded shape is neat and even. Apply glue onto the underside of the part A.

⑪Place the glued side on the base matching the four corners and press.

●**Actual-size Pattern for Ribbon Bow (B)**

⑫A complete work.

● **Actual-size Pattern for Package (A)**

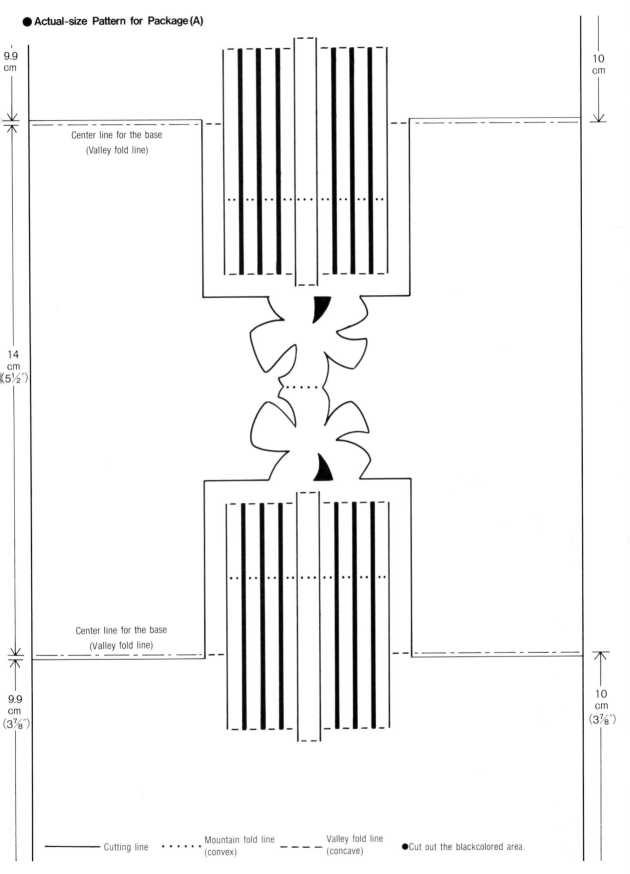

9.9 cm

10 cm

Center line for the base
(Valley fold line)

14 cm
($5\frac{1}{2}''$)

Center line for the base
(Valley fold line)

9.9 cm
($3\frac{7}{8}''$)

10 cm
($3\frac{7}{8}''$)

———— Cutting line   •••••• Mountain fold line
(convex)   – – – – Valley fold line
(concave)   ●Cut out the blackcolored area.

31

(18) **Circling,** *shown on page 14.*

●**Actual-size Patterns**   Cut 1 each

Prepare the following materials. (a) Kent paper for circles, 16cm by 22cm ($6\frac{1}{4}'' \times 8\frac{5}{8}''$). (b) Kent paper for the base, 10cm by 15cm ($3\frac{7}{8}'' \times 5\frac{7}{8}''$), 2 sheets. (c) Kent paper for backing, 10cm by 15cm ($3\frac{7}{8}'' \times 5\frac{7}{8}''$), 2 sheets. (d) Japanese rice paper for joint and reinforcement, 3cm by 15cm ($1\frac{1}{8}'' \times 5\frac{7}{8}''$). (e) Cotton thread. (f) Patterns for circles.

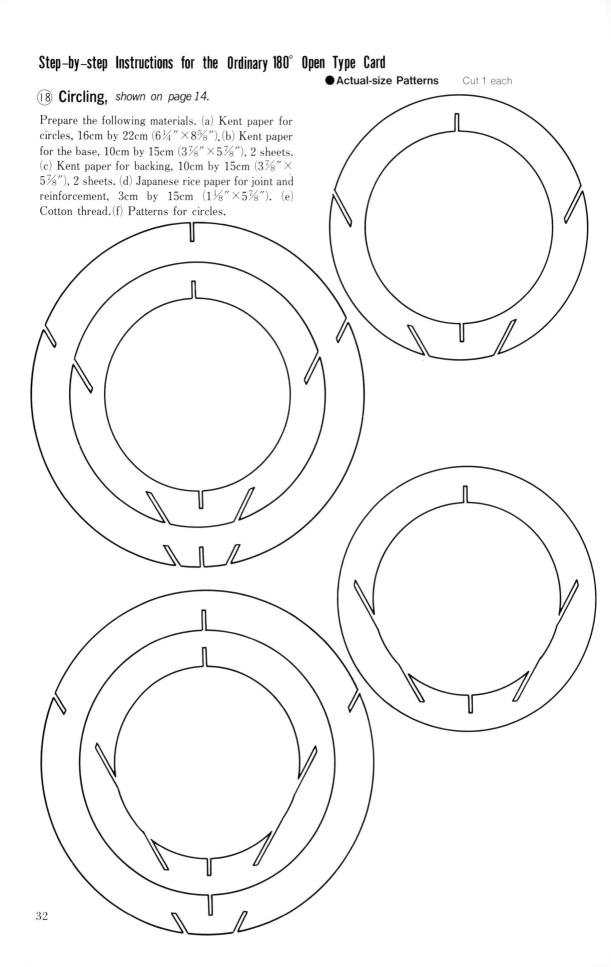

①Cut out the required number of circles using a circle cutter.

②Place the circles on the traced patterns and mark the slits for joints. Cut out the slits.

③Check whether all the joints are cut out.

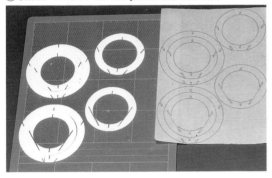

④Assemble the circles starting with the bigger ones.

⑤Carefully join the circles together matching the joints.

⑥To match the joints of the outer circles at the bottom, gently bend the circles.

⑦After all the circles have been assembled, flatten the circles as shown in the photo and check whether they are easy to open up.

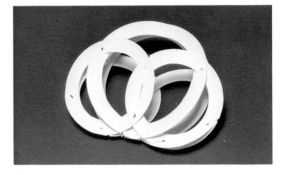

⑧Open up and place circles upside down. Insert cotton thread into slits and tie ends (see page 35).

33

⑨Repeat for the left side.

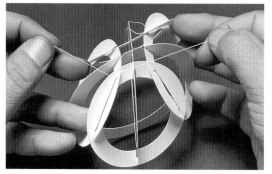

⑩Make the base. Apply glue onto Japanese rice paper for joint of the base.

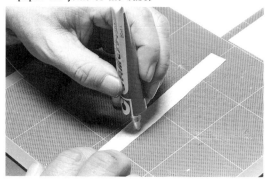

⑪Place two sheets of Kent paper on the glued Japanese rice paper. Before the glue is completely dry, fold the base in half.

⑫Make two holes in the base with a stylus pen.

⑬Insert each end of thread into the hole using a stylus pen.

⑭Pull thread and fix it temporarily with drafting tape.

⑮Check the shape of circles, tension of thread and opening of the card. Reshape if necessary.

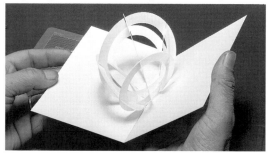

⑯Remove the drafting tape and glue small pieces of Japanese rice paper to fix the thread. Glue Kent paper onto the underside of the base for backing.

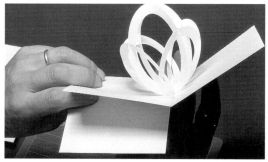

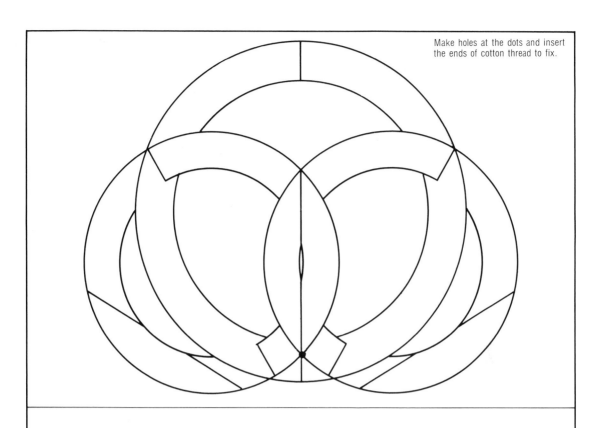

Make holes at the dots and insert
the ends of cotton thread to fix.

The finished card.

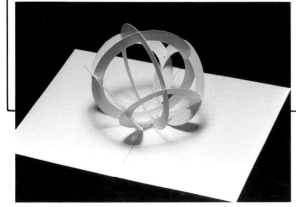

Instructions and Actual-size Patterns.

①**OSAKA Castle,** *shown on page 5.*

——— Cutting line • • • • • Mountain fold line (convex) — — — Valley fold line (concave)

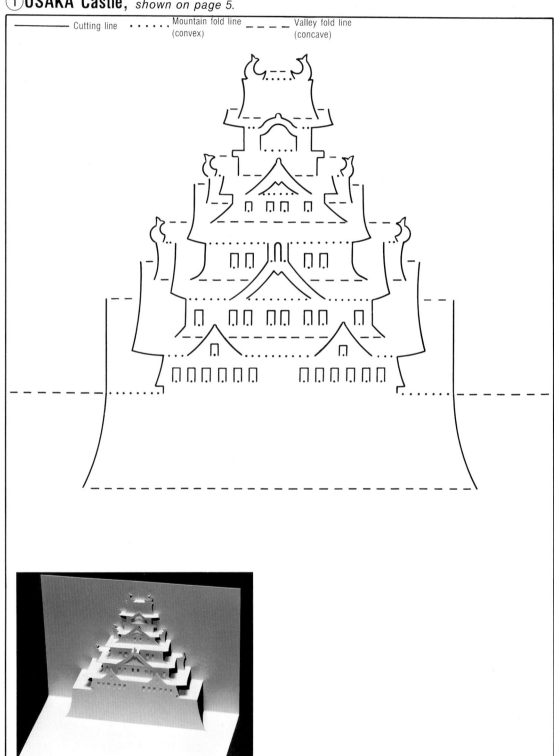

②HIMEJI Castle, *shown on page 5.*

——— Cutting line　• • • • • Mountain fold line　— — — Valley fold line　● Cut out the blackcolored area.
(convex)　　　　　(concave)

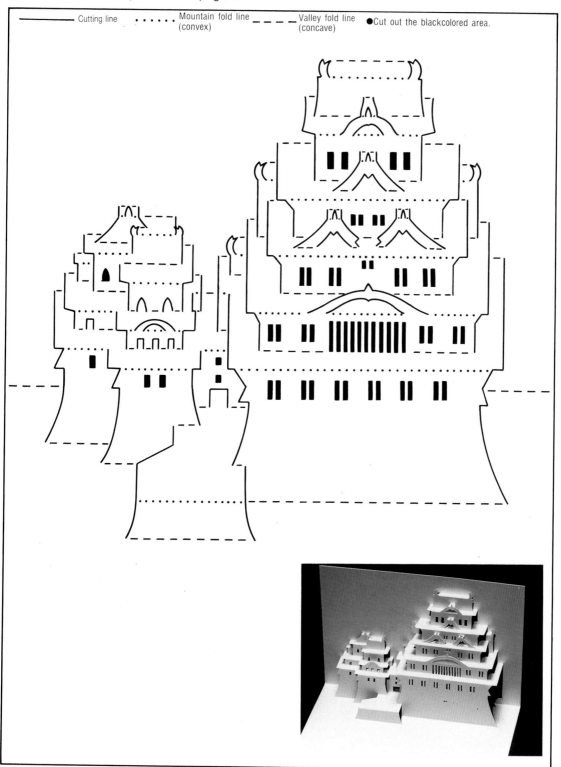

③ **NAGOYA Castle,** *shown on page 6.*

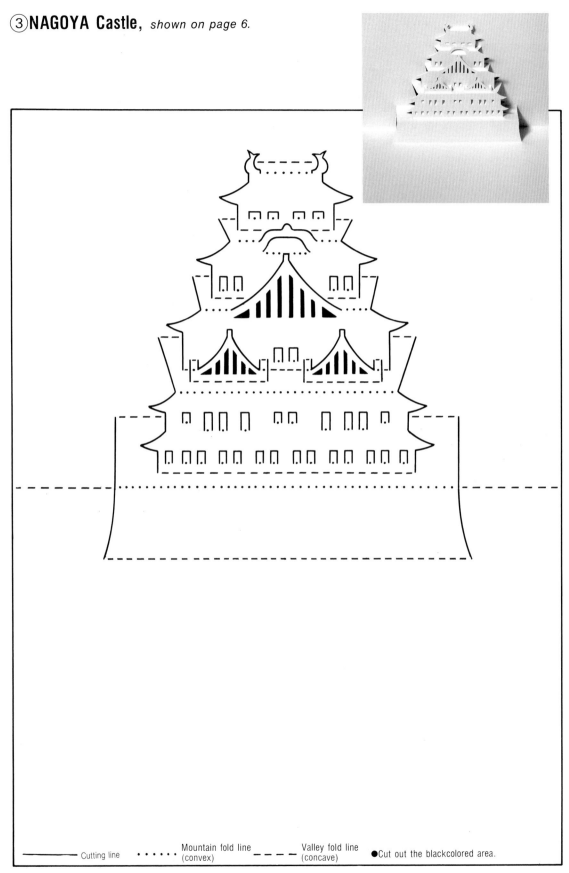

Cutting line ・・・・・・ Mountain fold line (convex) ⎯ ⎯ ⎯ Valley fold line (concave) ●Cut out the blackcolored area.

⑤Chateau Chenonceau, *shown on page 7.*

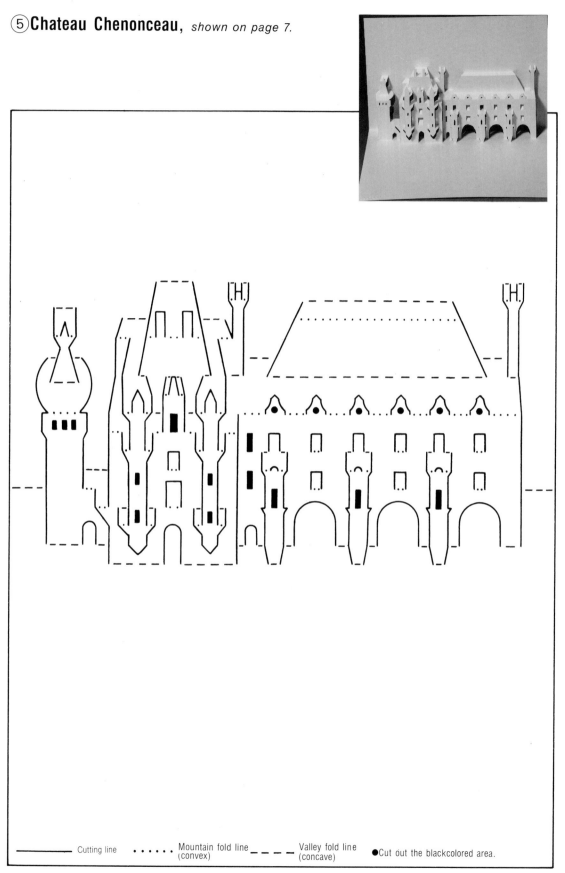

—— Cutting line • • • • • Mountain fold line (convex) _ _ _ _ Valley fold line (concave) ●Cut out the blackcolored area.

⑥Chateau d'Azay-le-Rideau,

shown on page 7.

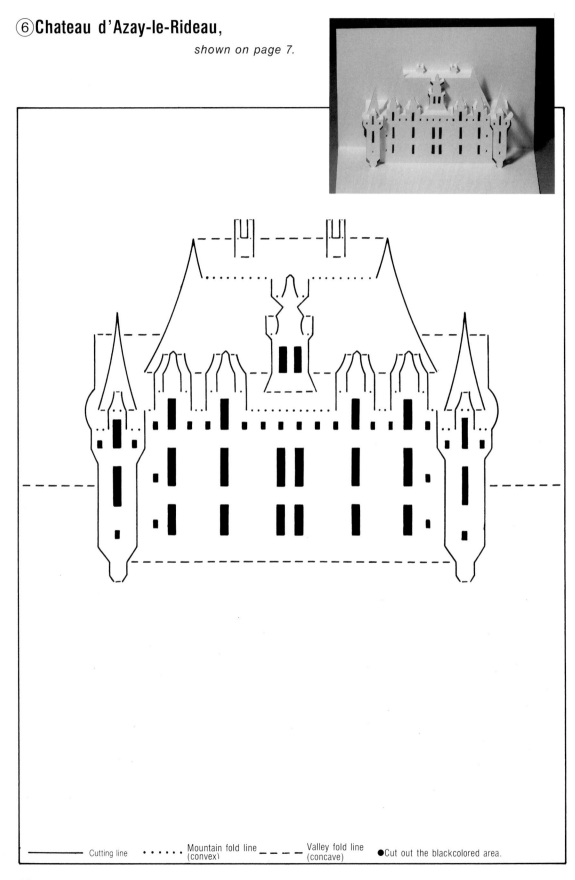

⑦ Schloss Neuschwanstein, *shown on page 7.*

Cutting line   • • • • • Mountain fold line (convex)   ‒ ‒ ‒ Valley fold line (concave)   ●Cut out the blackcolored area.

Milano Duomo, *shown on page 8.*

———— Cutting line ・・・・・ Mountain fold line (convex) ––– Valley fold line (concave)

⑨ **Salon Rico,** *shown on page 8.*

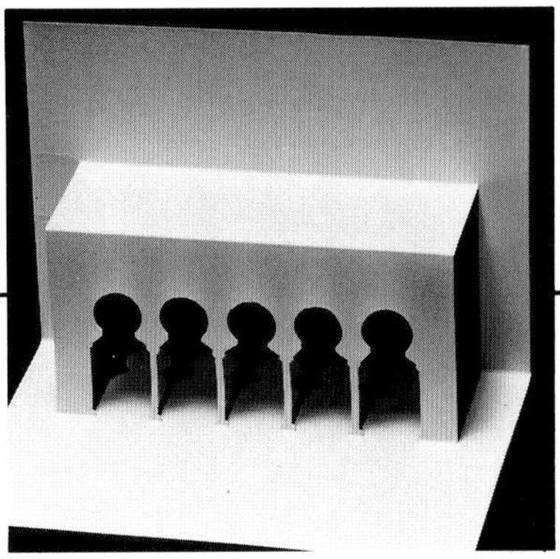

Cutting line · · · · · · Mountain fold line (convex) – – – – Valley fold line (concave)

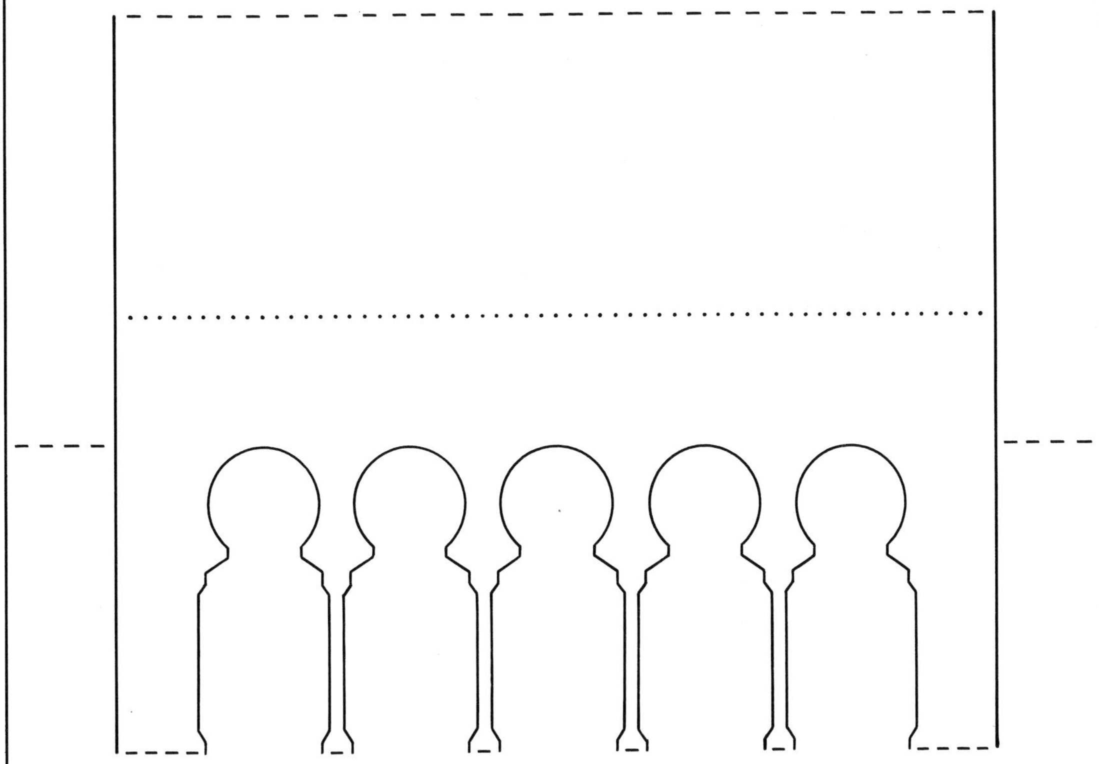

⑩Alhambra Granada Court of Lions, *shown on page 8.*

——— Cutting line　• • • • • • Mountain fold line (convex)　– – – Valley fold line (concave)

⑫ **Medina,** *shown on page 9.*

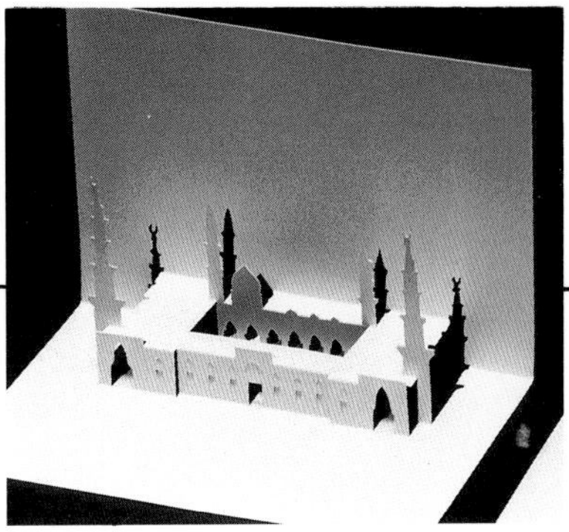

Cutting line ...... Mountain fold line (convex) – – – – Valley fold line (concave)

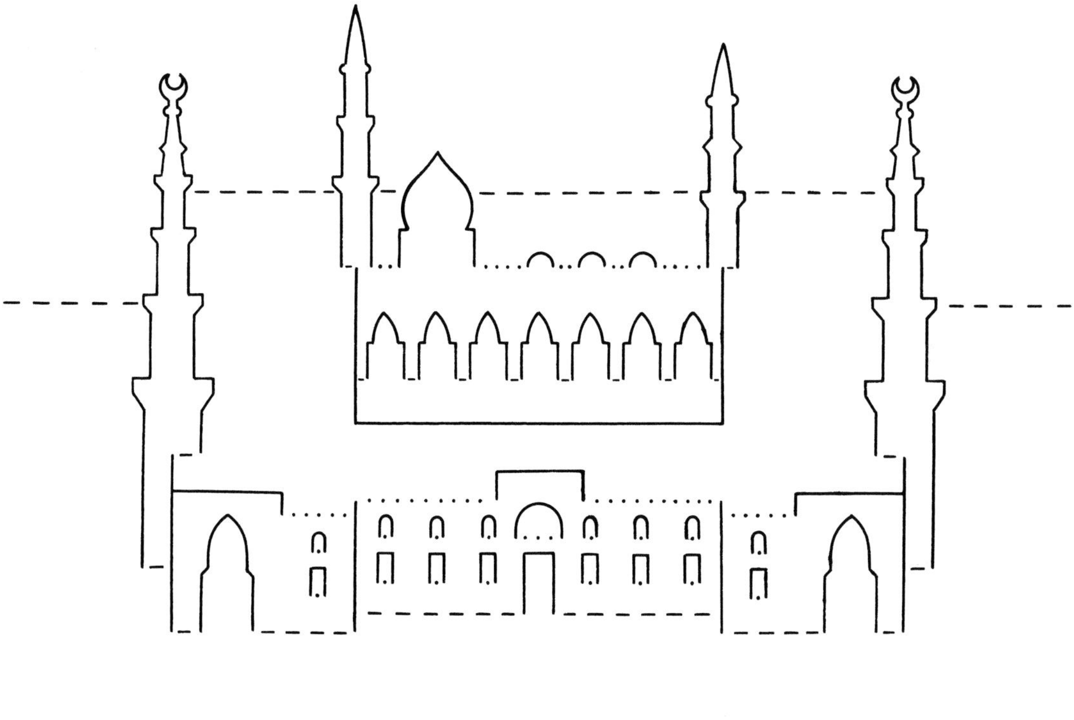

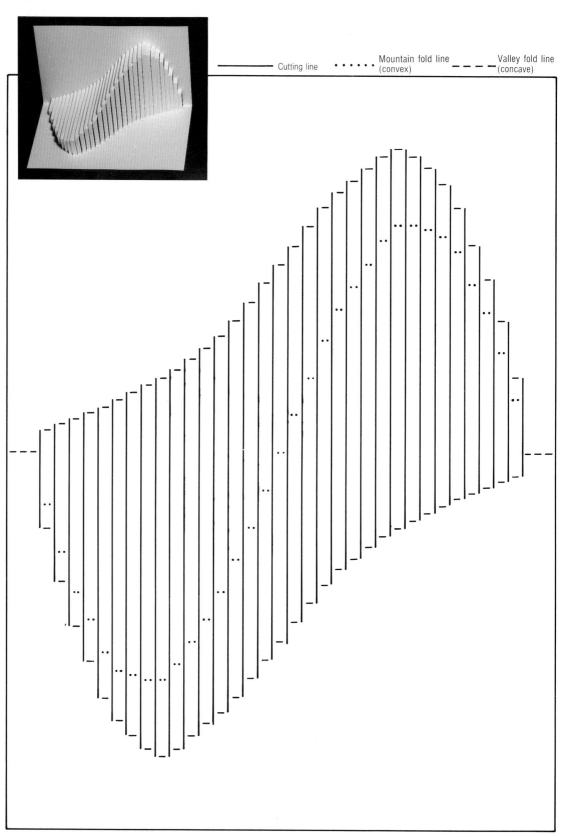

Cutting line
• • • • • Mountain fold line
(convex)
– – – – Valley fold line
(concave)

(16) **Volcano A,** *shown on page 11.*

——— Cutting line · · · · · · Mountain fold line (convex) – – – Valley fold line (concave)

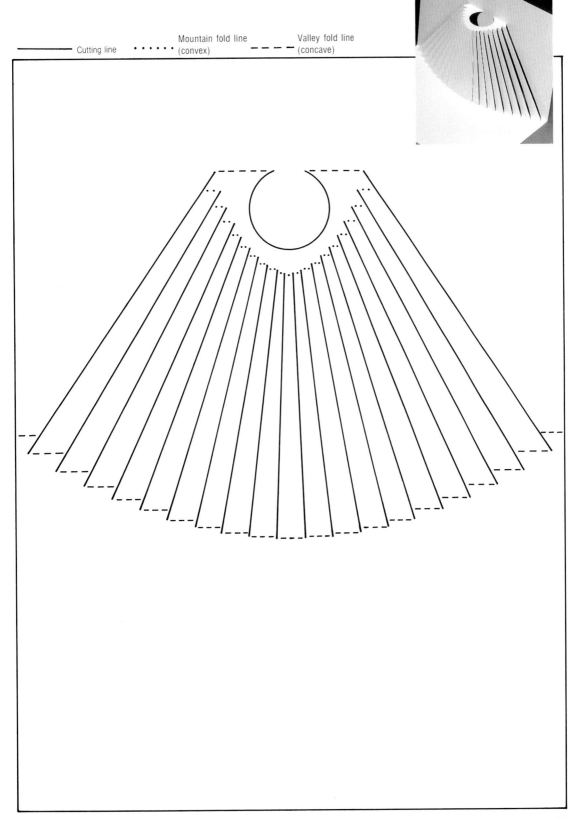

Cutting line ••••••Mountain fold line (convex) ‒ ‒ ‒Valley fold line (concave)

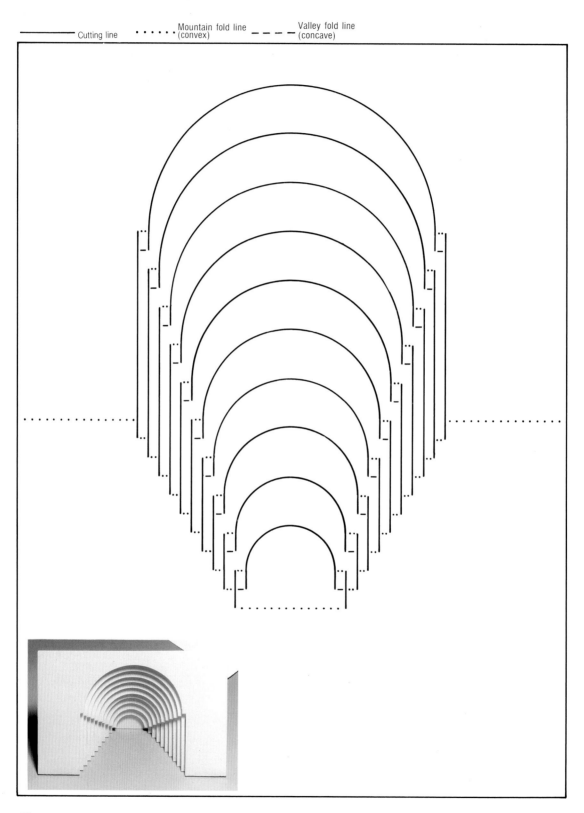

⑲Cedars, *shown on page 12.*

● **Patterns for Cedars
(Actual-size)**

Cut out one piece each for A, B, C and D. Assemble A and B together,
then C and D. Assemble two pairs together. Attach thread at the
marked places and fix onto the base.

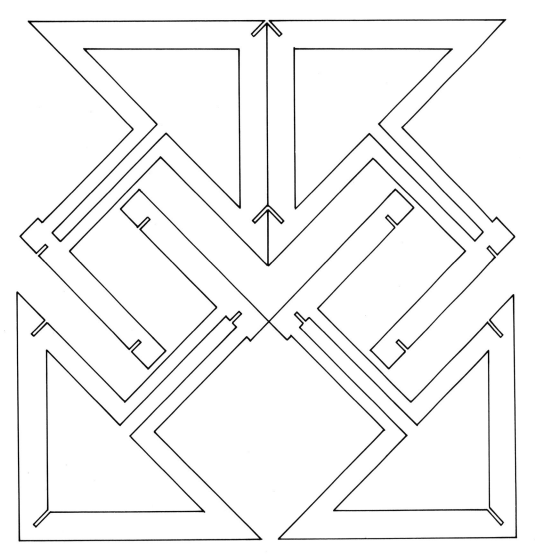

● Diagram for Unfolding (Actual-size)

Make holes at the dots and insert
the ends of cotton thread to fix.

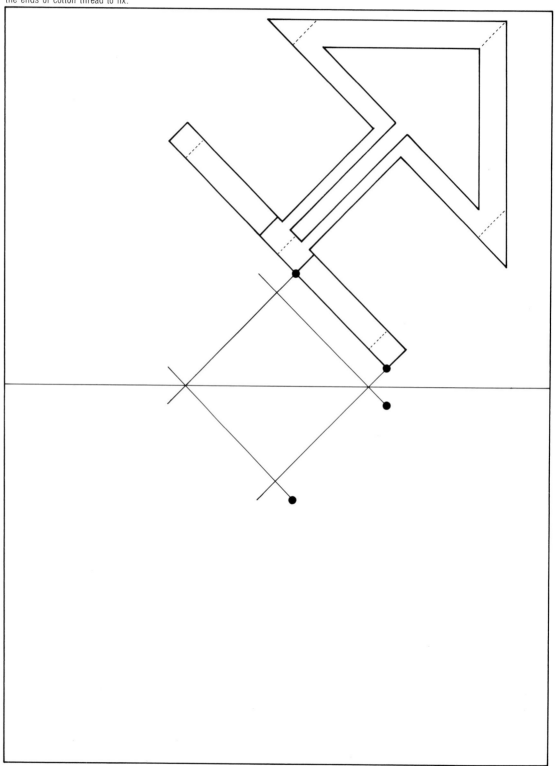

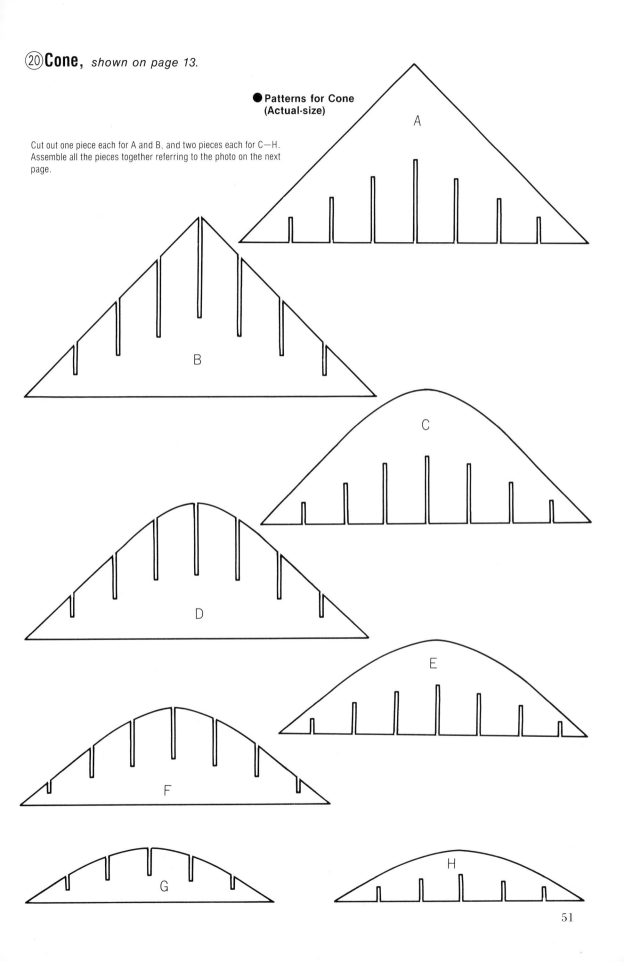

⑳ Cone, *shown on page 13.*

● **Patterns for Cone
(Actual-size)**

Cut out one piece each for A and B, and two pieces each for C—H.
Assemble all the pieces together referring to the photo on the next
page.

A

B

C

D

E

F

G

H

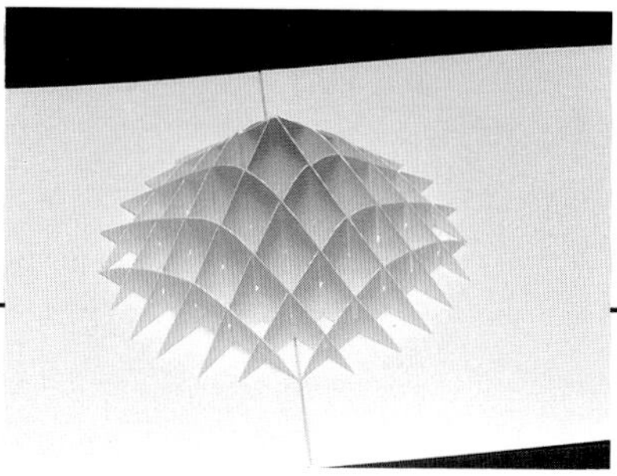

● Diagram for Unfolding (Actual-size)

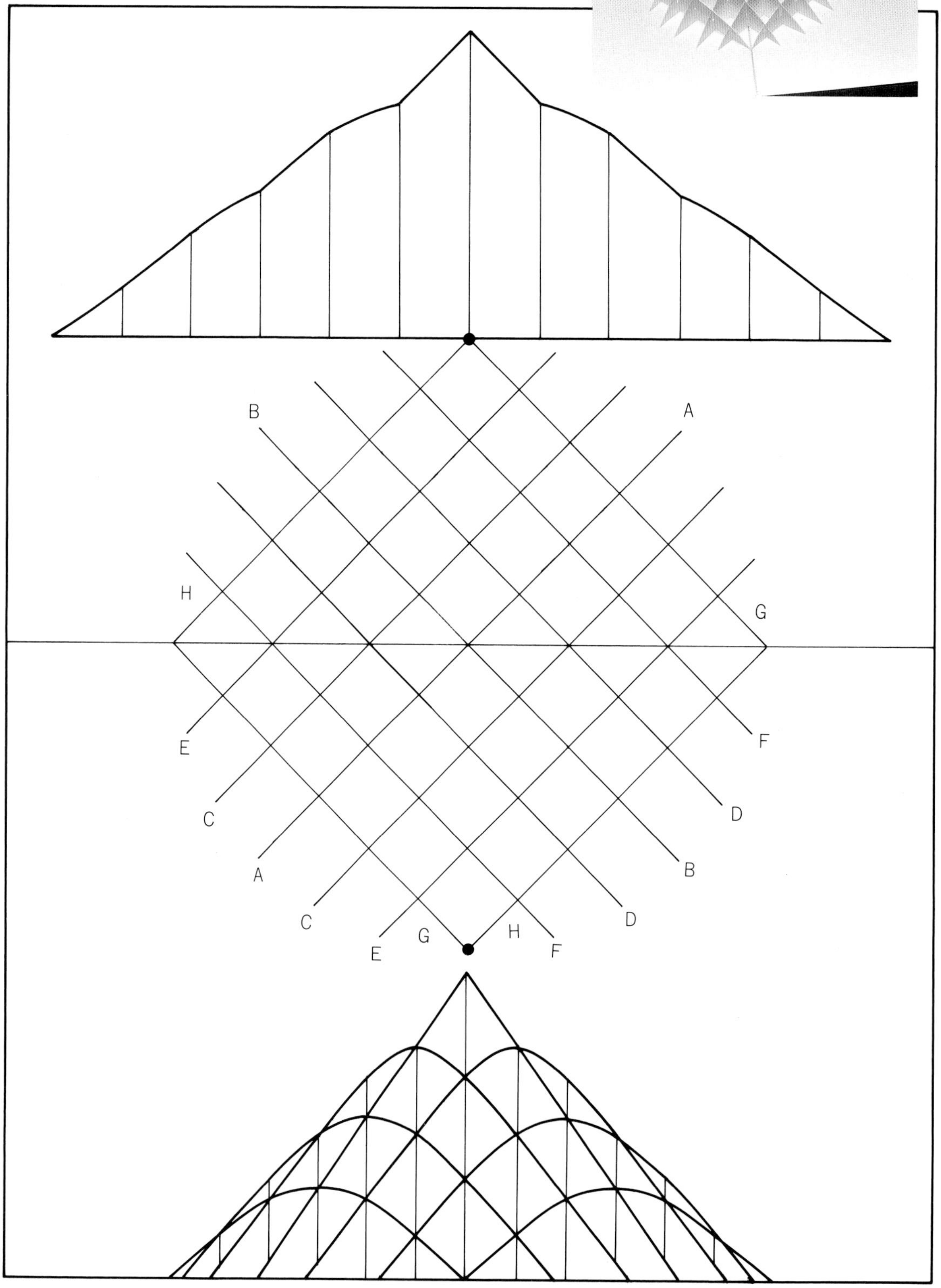

B   A

H   G

E   F

C   D

A   B

C   G   H   D
E   F

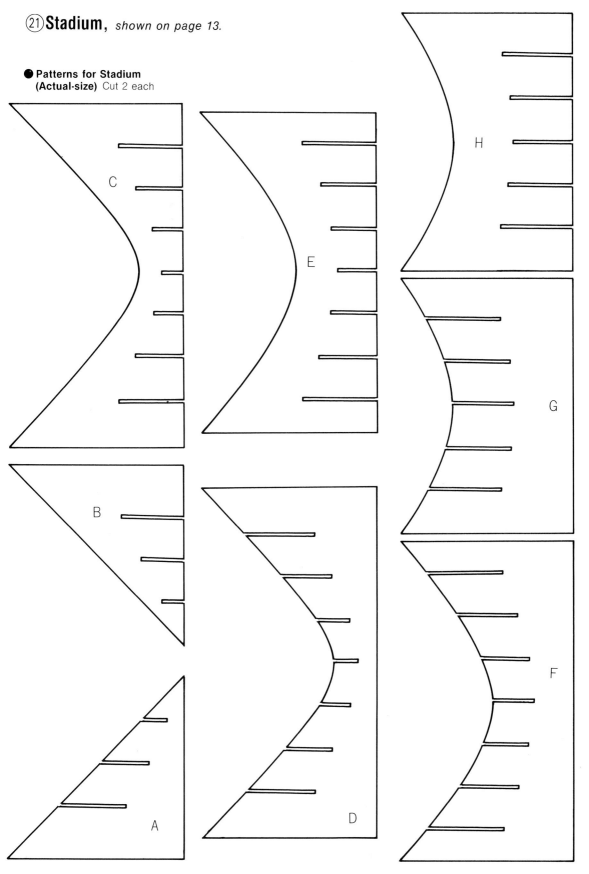

(21) **Stadium,** *shown on page 13.*

● **Patterns for Stadium**
  (Actual-size) Cut 2 each

C

E

H

B

D

G

A

F

● Diagram for Unfolding (Actual-size)

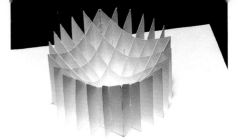

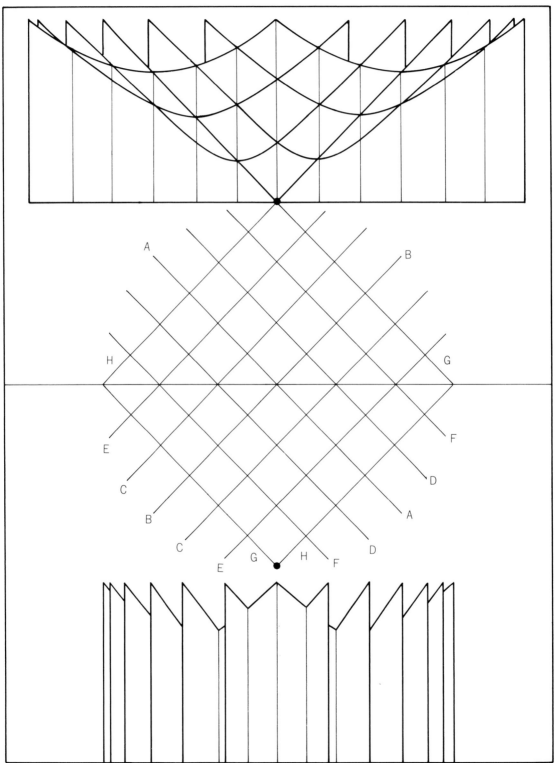

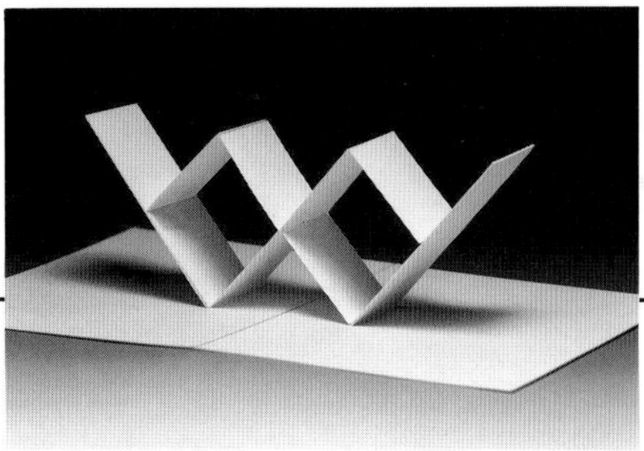

●**Patterns and Diagram for Unfolding (Actual-size)**

Cut out two pieces for A (plus two more pieces for backing), one piece each for B and C, and two pieces for D. Assemble B and C. Join A and D. D and C, D and B, B and A, and C and A using small pieces of Japanese rice paper for joints. Attach thread and fix onto the base.

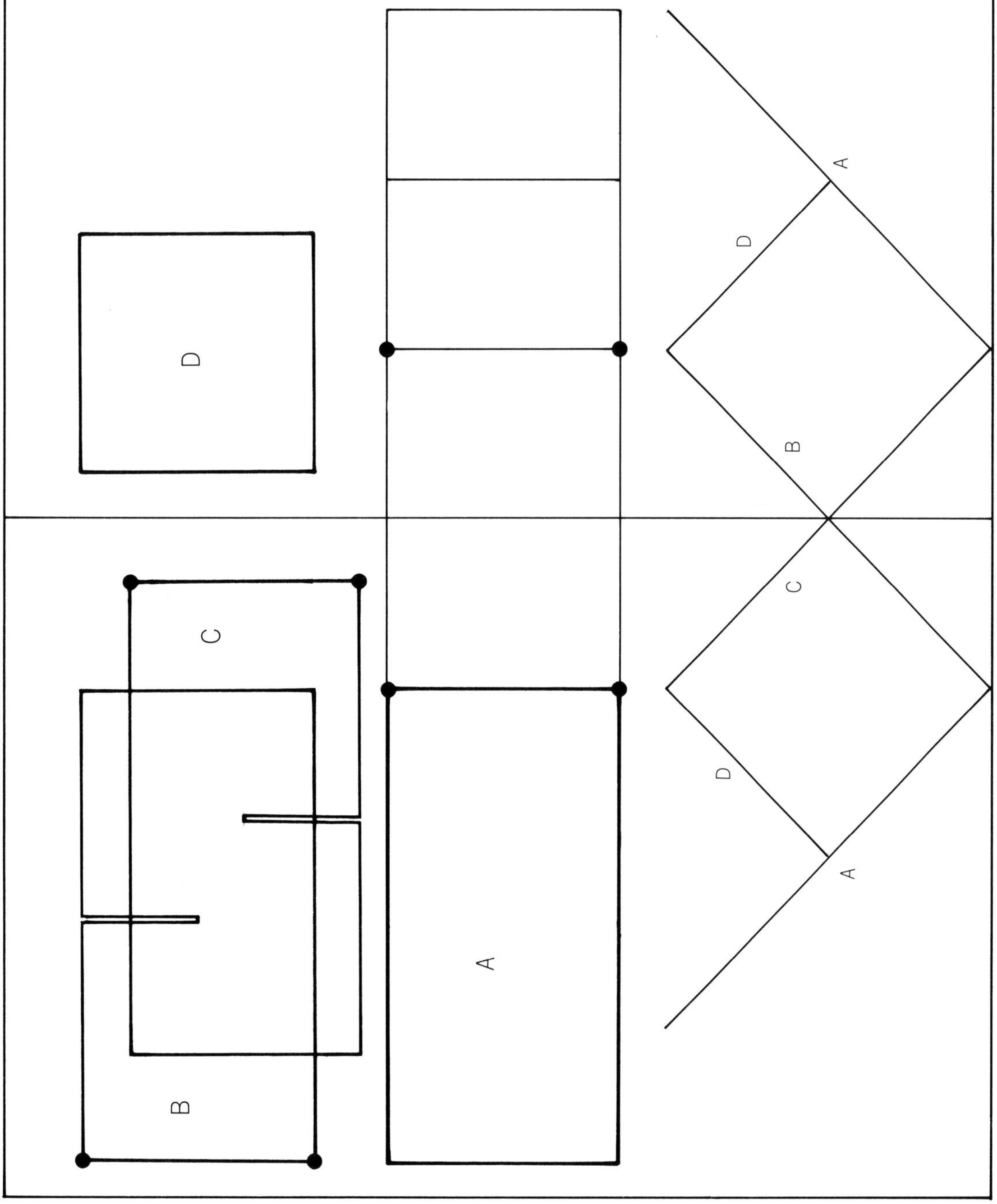

D

A

D

B

C

C

D

A

A

C

B

B

A

● **Patterns and Diagram for Unfolding (Actual-size)**

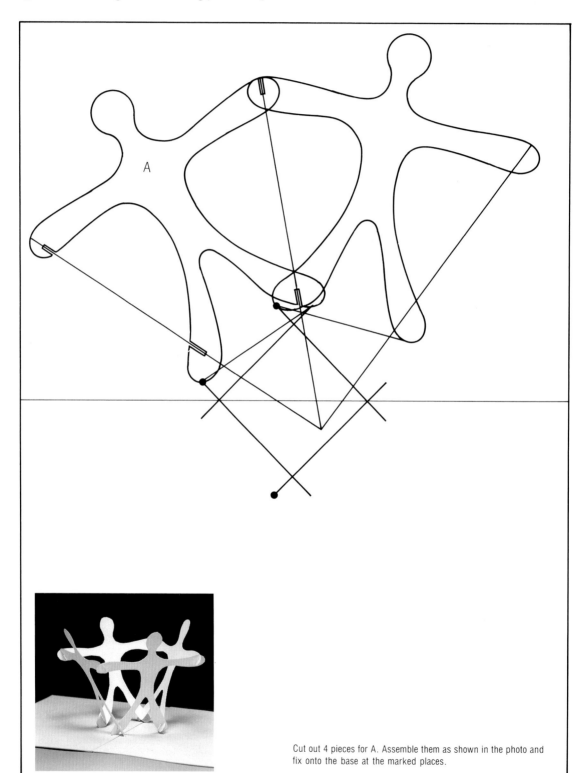

A

Cut out 4 pieces for A. Assemble them as shown in the photo and fix onto the base at the marked places.

●**Patterns and Diagram for Unfolding (Actual-size)**

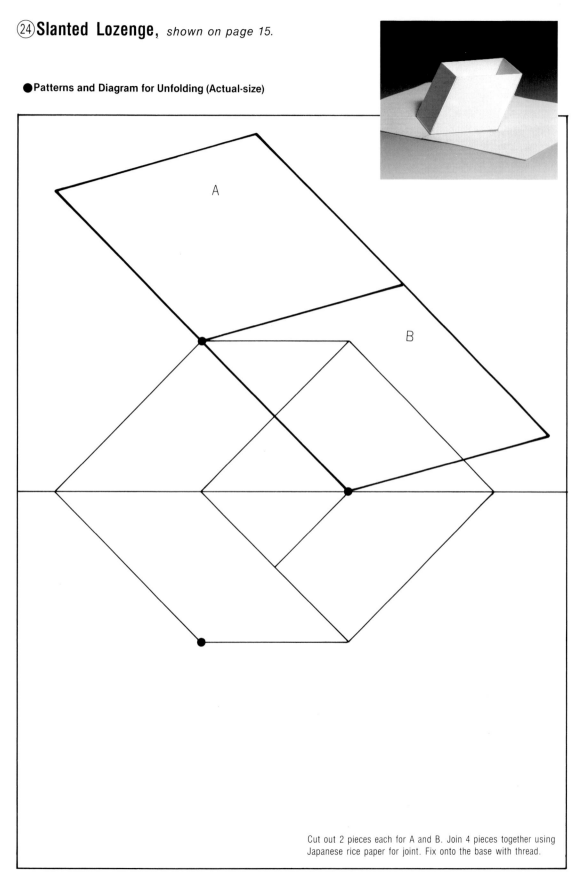

A

B

Cut out 2 pieces each for A and B. Join 4 pieces together using
Japanese rice paper for joint. Fix onto the base with thread.

● **Patterns and Diagram for Unfolding (Actual-size)**

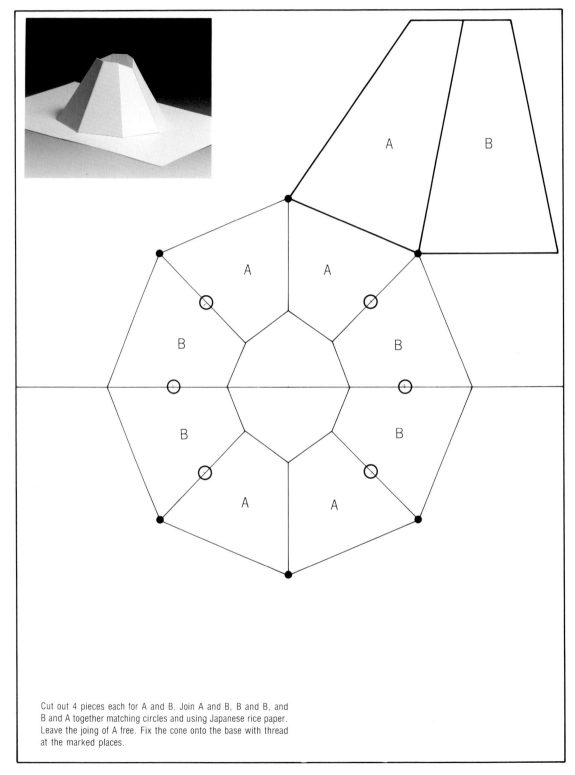

Cut out 4 pieces each for A and B. Join A and B, B and B, and
B and A together matching circles and using Japanese rice paper.
Leave the joing of A free. Fix the cone onto the base with thread
at the marked places.

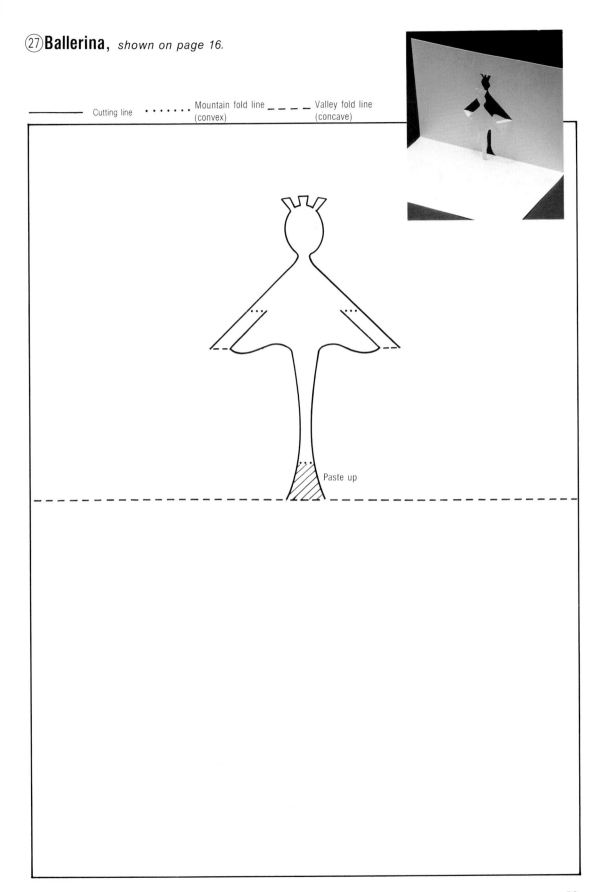

——————— Cutting line　• • • • • • •　Mountain fold line　_ _ _ _ _　Valley fold line
　　　　　　　　　　　　　　　　　(convex)　　　　　　　　(concave)

Paste up

㉘ Tree of Life, *shown on page 16.*

MATERIALS: One sheet of Kent paper for the base, 15 by 20cm (5⅞″×7⅞″). One sheet of Kent paper for parts, 15 by 20cm (5⅞″×7⅞″). 2 sheets of Kent paper for backing, 15 by 10cm (5⅞″×3⅞″). Japanese rice paper and sewing thread.

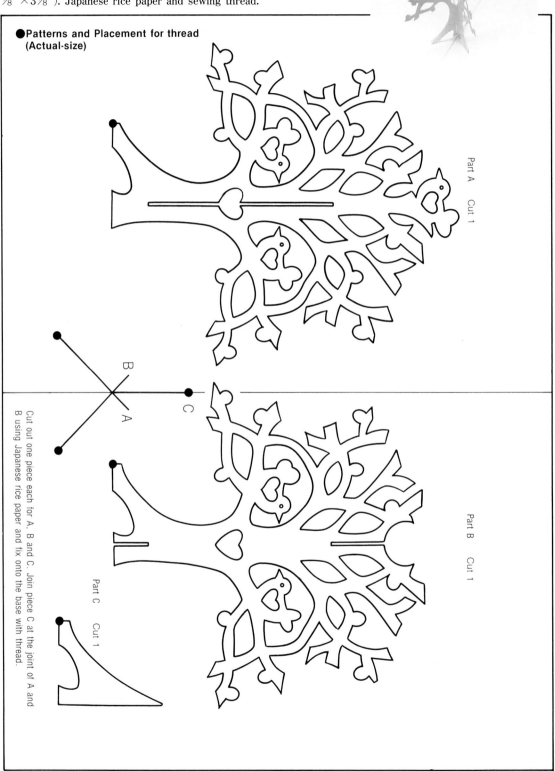

● **Patterns and Placement for thread (Actual-size)**

Part A   Cut 1

Part B   Cut 1

Part C   Cut 1

Cut out one piece each for A, B and C. Join piece C at the joint of A and B using Japanese rice paper and fix onto the base with thread.

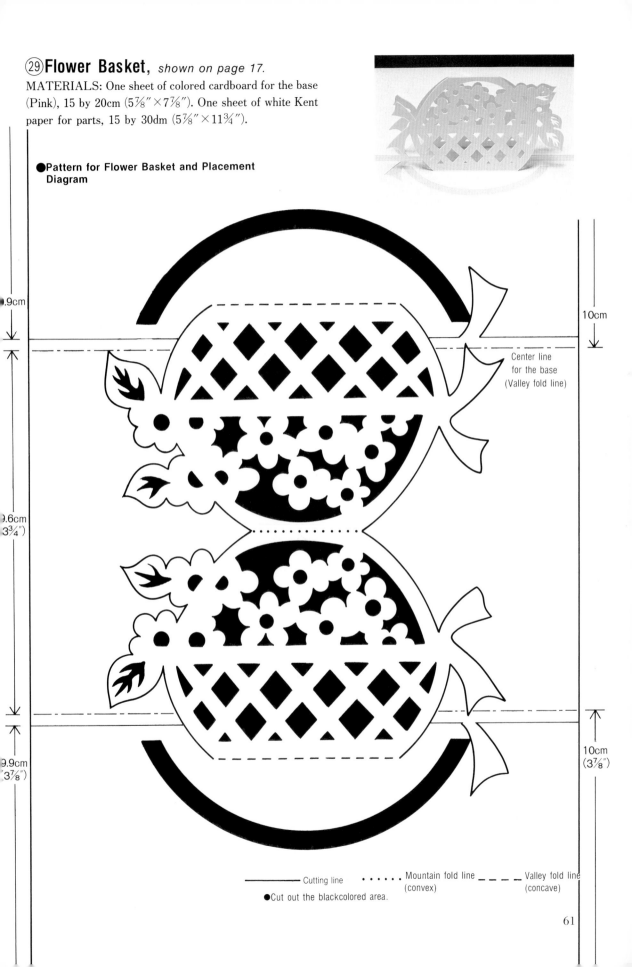

㉙Flower Basket, *shown on page 17.*

MATERIALS: One sheet of colored cardboard for the base (Pink), 15 by 20cm (5⅞″×7⅞″). One sheet of white Kent paper for parts, 15 by 30dm (5⅞″×11¾″).

●**Pattern for Flower Basket and Placement Diagram**

9.9cm

10cm

Center line
for the base
(Valley fold line)

9.6cm
(3¾″)

9.9cm
(3⅞″)

10cm
(3⅞″)

————— Cutting line • • • • • Mountain fold line _ _ _ Valley fold line
(convex) (concave)
●Cut out the blackcolored area.

61

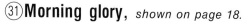

㉛ Morning glory, *shown on page 18.*

MATERIALS: One sheet of colored cardboard for parts, 15 by 20cm (5⅞″×7⅞″). One sheet of cardboard in same color with parts for the base, 15 by 20cm (5⅞″×7⅞″). One sheet of Kent paper for backing, 15 by 20cm (5⅞″×7⅞″). Japanese rice paper and sewing thread.

● **Patterns and Placement for thread (Actual-size)**

Cut out one piece each for the pistil
(One more piece each for backing)

Cut out 4 stems
(Cut out 4 more for backing)

Petal C

Petal D

Petal B

Petal A

Cut out one piece each for the petals A, B, C and D (one more piece each for backing).
Join the petal and the stem using Japanese rice paper. Make 4 sets.
Join A and D, and B and C indivisually with Japanese rice paper. Attach thread onto the points of A and B, and C and D.
Glue pieces for backing onto the underside of the petals and fix thread onto the base. Place the pistil at center and fix with thread.

㉜**Tulip,** *shown on page 18.*

MATERIALS: One sheet of colored cardboard for parts, 12 by 22cm (8¾″×8 ⅝″). One sheet of cardboard in same color with parts for the base, 15 by 20cm (5⅞″× 7⅞″). One sheet of Kent paper for backing, 15 by 20cm (5⅞″×7⅞″). Japanese rice-paper and sewing thread.

●**Patterns and Placement for thread**
(Actual-size)

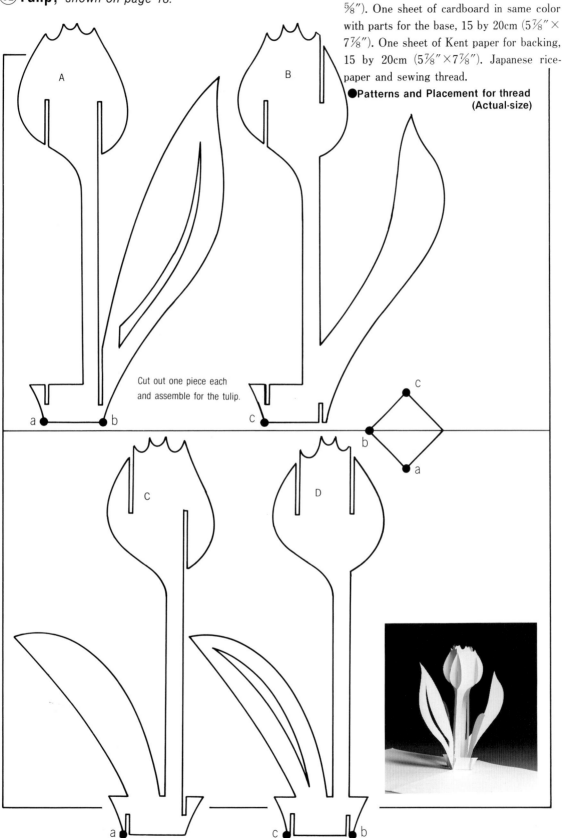

A

B

Cut out one piece each
and assemble for the tulip.

a ● ● b

C ●

c ● ● b

C

C

b ● ● a

D

a ●

c ● ● b

———— Cutting line · · · · · Mountain fold line (convex) – – – Valley fold line (concave)

35 **Sunflower,** *shown on page 19.*

MATERIALS: One sheet of colored cardboard for the parts, 15 by 30cm (5⅞″×11¾″). One sheet of cardboard in same color with parts for the base, 15 by 20cm (5⅞″×7⅞″). One sheet of Kent paper for backing, 15 by 20cm (5⅞″×7⅞″). Japanese rice paper and sewing thread.

● **Patterns and Placement for thread (Actual-size)**

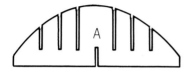

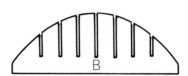

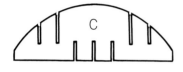

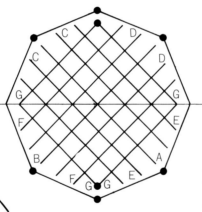

Cut out one piece each for A and B, 2 pieces each for C, D, E and F and 4 pieces for G. Cut out 8 pieces each for H and I. Join them together with Japanese rice paper to make the outer and inner petals.
Assemble all the pieces and fix them onto the base with thread.

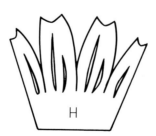

㉞ Camellia, *shown on page 19.*

MATERIALS: One sheet of colored cardboard for the parts, 20 by 30cm ($7\frac{7}{8}'' \times 11\frac{3}{4}''$). One sheet of cardboard in same color with parts for the base, 15 by 20cm ($5\frac{7}{8}'' \times 7\frac{7}{8}''$). One sheet of Kent paper for backing, 15 by 20cm ($5\frac{7}{8}'' \times 7\frac{7}{8}''$). Japanese rice paper and sewing thread.

● **Placement for thread (Actual-size)**

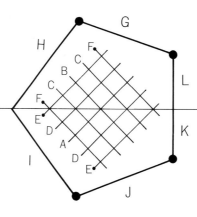

Join the petals with Japanese rice paper following the diagram and attach the backed petals to the base with thread.

Assemble the pistil following the diagram and attach to the base with thread

66

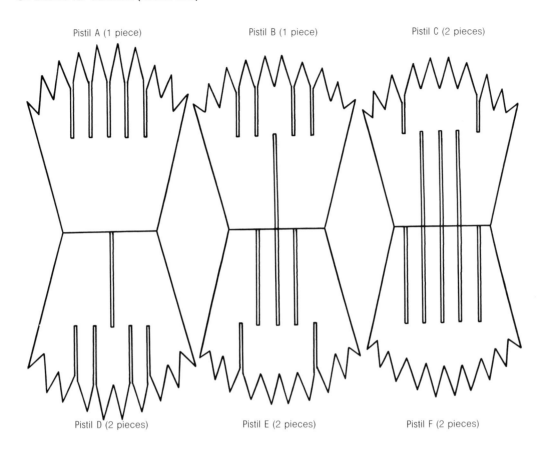

Pistil A (1 piece)   Pistil B (1 piece)   Pistil C (2 pieces)

Pistil D (2 pieces)   Pistil E (2 pieces)   Pistil F (2 pieces)

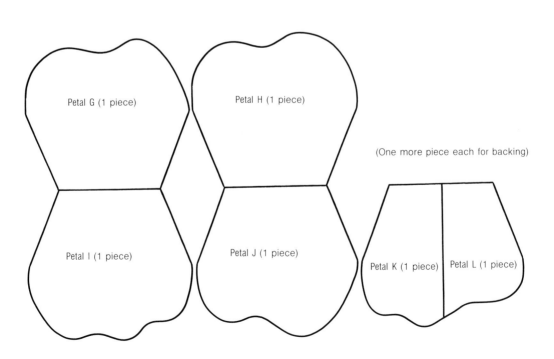

Petal G (1 piece)   Petal H (1 piece)

(One more piece each for backing)

Petal I (1 piece)   Petal J (1 piece)   Petal K (1 piece)   Petal L (1 piece)

㊱Rabbit A,

shown on page 20.

MATERIALS: One sheet of Kent paper for parts, 10 by 50cm ($3\frac{7}{8}'' \times 19\frac{5}{8}''$). One sheet of colored cardboard for the base, 10 by 30cm ($3\frac{7}{8}'' \times 11\frac{3}{4}''$).

● **Pattern for Rabbit and Placement Diagram**

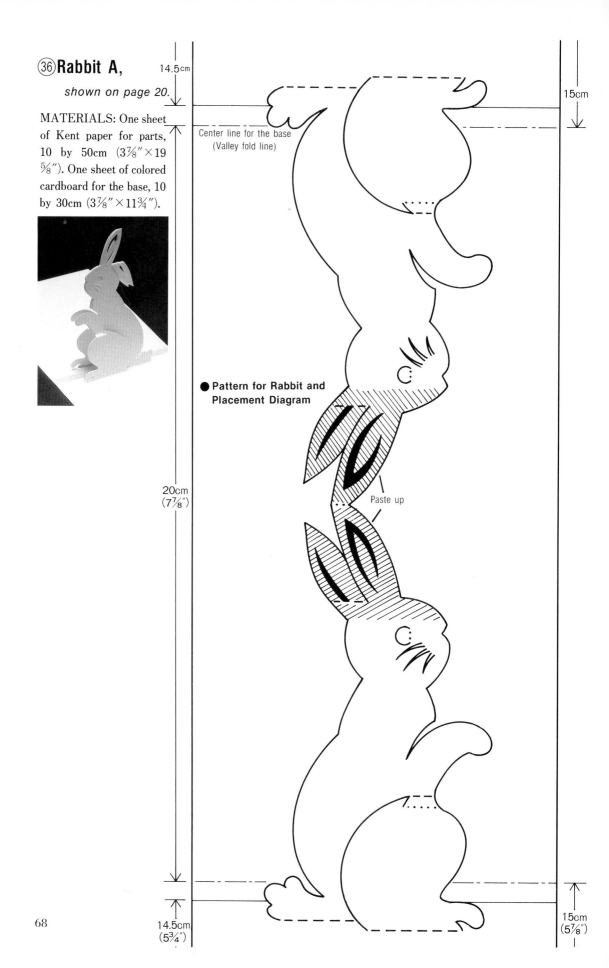

14.5cm

15cm

Center line for the base
(Valley fold line)

20cm
($7\frac{7}{8}''$)

Paste up

14.5cm
($5\frac{3}{4}''$)

15cm
($5\frac{7}{8}''$)

㊲ Crane & Pine,

shown on page 20.

MATERIALS: One sheet of Kent paper for parts, 10 by 50cm(3⅞″×19 ⅝″). One sheet of colored cardboard for the base, 10 by 30cm (3⅞″×11 ¾″).

The pattern at left is ten-twelfths actual size. Enlarge the pattern when making the card.

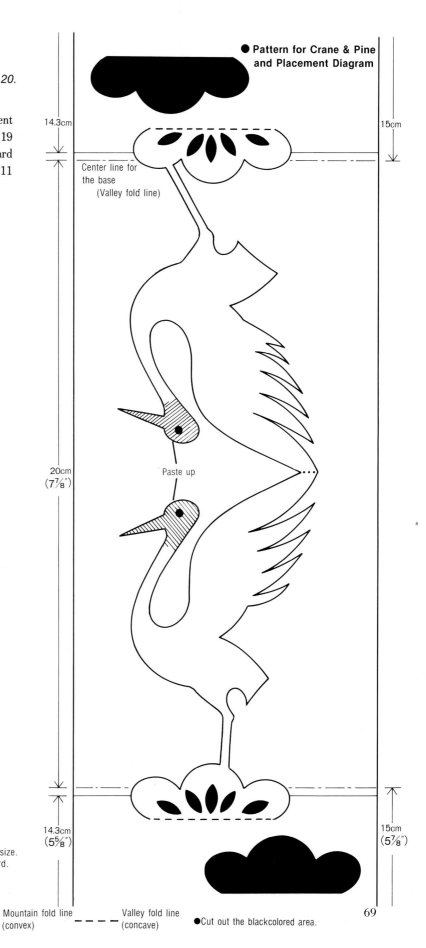

● **Pattern for Crane & Pine and Placement Diagram**

14.3cm

15cm

Center line for the base
(Valley fold line)

20cm
(7⅞″)

Paste up

14.3cm
(5⅝″)

15cm
(5⅞″)

——— Cutting line　　•••••• Mountain fold line (convex)　　――― Valley fold line (concave)　　●Cut out the black-colored area.

69

㊳Butterfly, *shown on page 20.*

MATERIALS: One sheet of Kent paper for parts, 15 by 33cm (5⅞″×13″). One sheet of Kent paper for the base, 15 by 20cm (5⅞″×7⅞″).

● **Pattern for Butterfly and Placement Diagram**

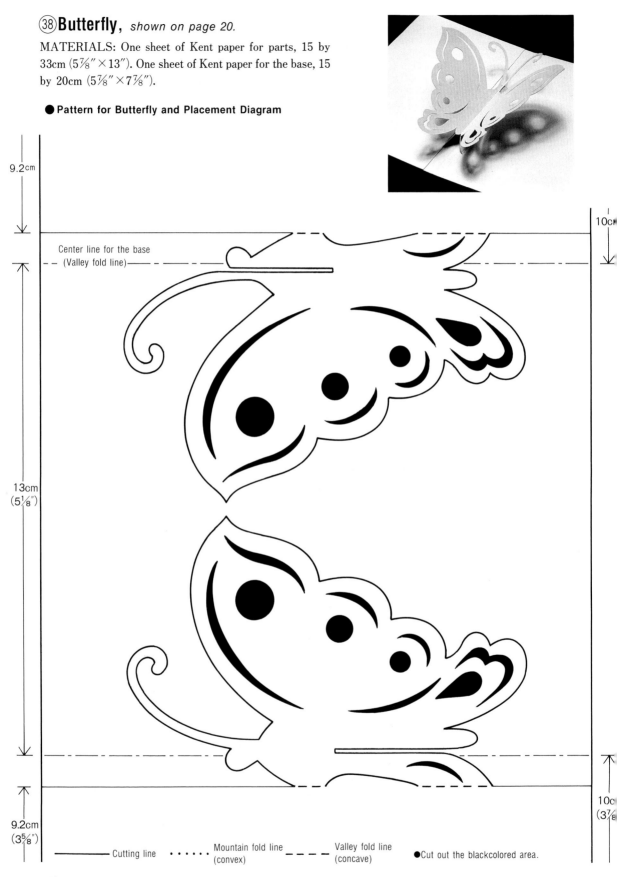

9.2cm

10cm

Center line for the base
(Valley fold line)

13cm
(5⅛″)

10c
(3⅞

9.2cm
(3⅝″)

——— Cutting line   •••• Mountain fold line (convex)   - - - Valley fold line (concave)   ●Cut out the blackcolored area.

㊱ **Tiger,** *shown on page 21.*

15cm

Center

15cm
(5⅞")

———— Cutting line   •••••• Mountain fold line
(convex)   – – – – Valley fold line
(concave)

71

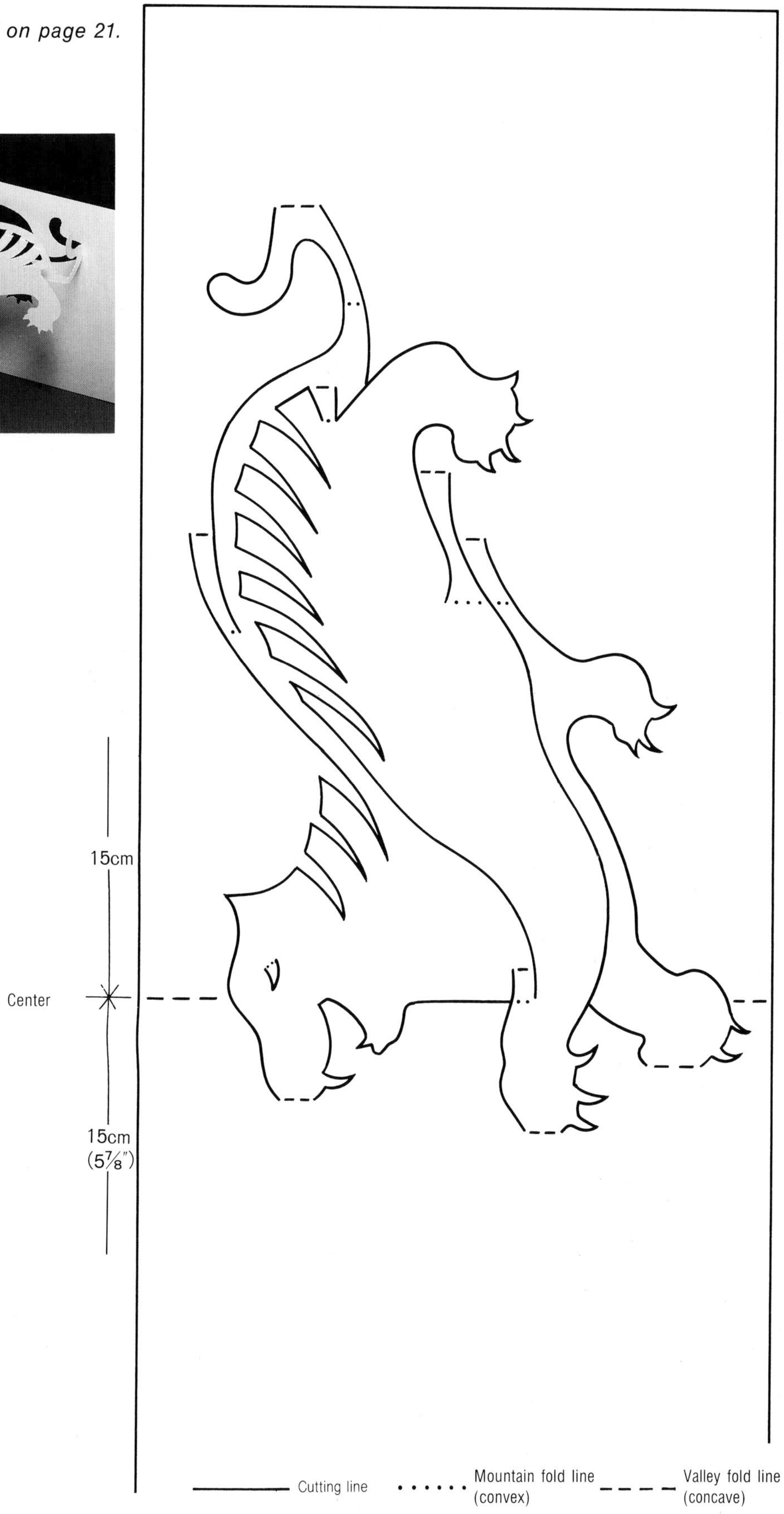

㊵Rabbit B, *shown on page 21.*

——————— Cutting line • • • • • • Mountain fold line (convex) – – – – Valley fold line (concave)

㊶Dragonfly, *shown on page 21.*

MATERIALS: One sheet of Kent paper for parts, 15 by 31cm (5⅞″ × 12¼″). One sheet of Kent paper for the base, 15 by 20cm (5⅞″ × 7⅞″).

●**Pattern for Dragonfly and Placement Diagram**

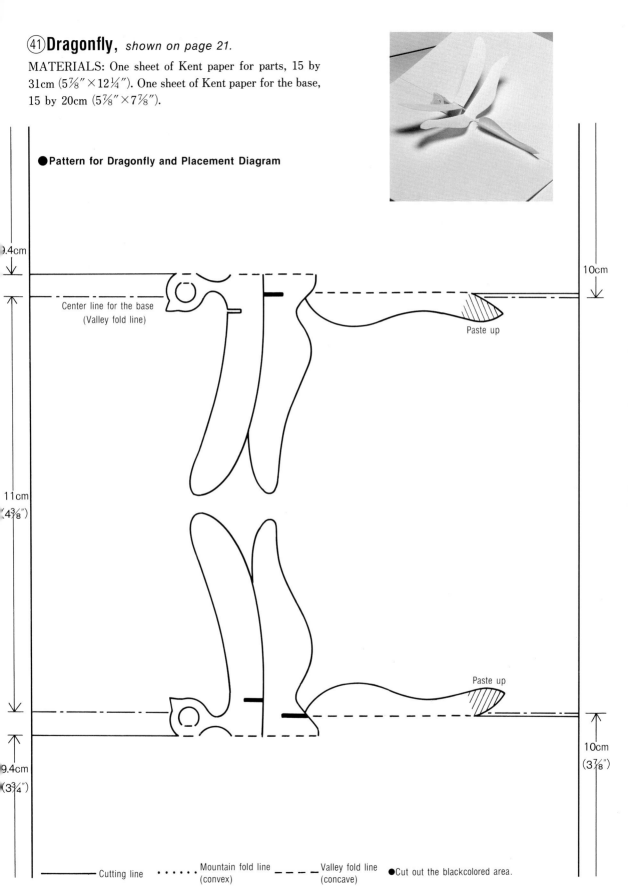

9.4cm

Center line for the base
(Valley fold line)

10cm

Paste up

11cm
(4⅜″)

Paste up

9.4cm
(3¾″)

10cm
(3⅞″)

—— Cutting line　• • • • • Mountain fold line   _ _ _ _ Valley fold line   ●Cut out the blackcolored area.
　　　　　　　　　　　　　　(convex)　　　　　　　　(concave)

73

㊷**JANUARY,** *shown on page 22.*

——— Cutting line ⋯⋯ Mountain fold line — — — Valley fold line
            (convex)   (concave)

JANUARY

——— Cutting line　• • • • • Mountain fold line　– – – – Valley fold line
(convex)　(concave)

——— Cutting line   • • • • • Mountain fold line _ _ _ _ Valley fold line
(convex)   (concave)

———— Cutting line   •••••• Mountain fold line ‗ ‗ ‗ ‗ Valley fold line
                          (convex)   (concave)

APRIL

(46)**MAY,** *shown on page 22.*

————— Cutting line   • • • • • Mountain fold line   – – – – Valley fold line
                              (convex)   (concave)

(47)**JUNE,** *shown on page 22.*

——— Cutting line • • • • • Mountain fold line (convex) — — — Valley fold line (concave)

JULY

————— Cutting line • • • • • Mountain fold line _ _ _ _ Valley fold line
                               (convex)   (concave)

AUGUST

——————— Cutting line • • • • • Mountain fold line (convex) — — — Valley fold line (concave)

SEPTEMBER

——— Cutting line   • • • • • Mountain fold line _ _ _ _ Valley fold line
                              (convex)   (concave)

OCTOBER

(52) NOVEMBER, *shown on page 23.*

—— Cutting line · · · · · · Mountain fold line (convex) – – – – Valley fold line (concave)

——— Cutting line   • • • • • • Mountain fold line   _ _ _ _ Valley fold line
(convex)   (concave)

DECEMBER

⑪ **Mecca,** *shown on page 9.*

——————— Cutting line
— — — — — Valley fold line (concave)
•••••••••• Mountain fold line (convex)

● Mountain-fold and Valley-fold lines are reversed in this diagram so that they cannot be seen on front. When you fold along the lines, the object will pop up on the reverse side.

⑭ Stairs, *shown on page 10.*

——————— Cutting line

— — — — — Valley fold line (concave)

• • • • • • • • Mountain fold line (convex)

●Mountain-fold and Valley-fold lines are reversed in this diagram so that they cannot be seen on front. When you fold along the lines, the object will pop up on the reverse side.

———————— Cutting line

– – – – – Valley fold line (concave)

• • • • • • • • Mountain fold line (convex)

●Mountain-fold and Valley-fold lines are reversed in this diagram so that they cannot be seen on front. When you fold along the lines, the object will pop up on the reverse side.

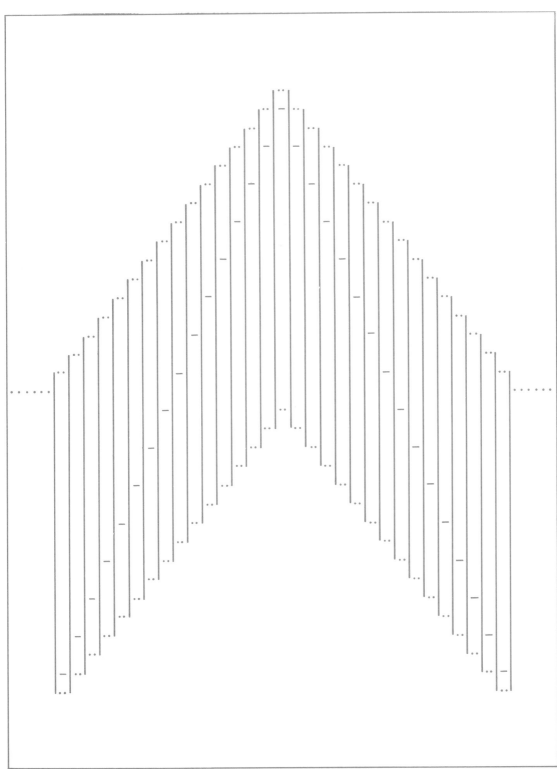

㉖Xmas Tree, *shown on page 16.*

—————— Cutting line
– – – – – Valley fold line (concave)
• • • • • • • Mountain fold line (convex)

●Mountain-fold and Valley-fold lines are reversed in this diagram so that they cannot be seen on front. When you fold along the lines, the object will pop up on the reverse side.